A Multiage Classroom

A Multiage Classroom
Choice and Possibility

Maureen McCann Miletta

HEINEMANN
Portsmouth, NH

Heinemann
A division of Reed Elsevier Inc.
361 Hanover Street
Portsmouth, NH 03801-3912
Offices and agents throughout the world

CIP is on file with the Library of Congress
0-435-08889-0

Editor: Toby Gordon
Production: Melissa L. Inglis
Cover design: Darci Mehall, Aureo Design
Manufacturing: Louise Richardson

Printed in the United States of America on acid-free paper
99 98 97 96   DA   1 2 3 4 5 6 7 8 9

For Aileen and Barbara

Contents

Foreword ix

Introduction xiii

Part I: Filling in the Background

One: *Initiative and Possibility* 3

Two: *A Community of Purposeful Learners* 15

Part II: Making Curricular Connections

Three: *Literacy and the Social Sciences* 27

Four: *Science and Mathematics* 43

Five: *The Arts* 57

Part III: Essential Elements

Six: *Cooperation and Shared Responsibility* 69

Seven: *Teaching Others to Teach* 79

Part IV: Assessment and Evaluation

Eight: *Student Assessment* 95

Nine: *Evaluation of the Program* 103

Appendix 111

References 119

Foreword

This is a book about open spaces, sunlit spaces, in which children are set free to pose their own questions and to choose the paths they will take to resolve them—and to keep moving on. It is difficult not to recall John Dewey writing in *My Pedagogic Creed*: "I believe that interests are the signs and symptoms of growing power. I believe that they represent dawning capacities. Accordingly, the constant and careful observation of interests is of the utmost importance for the educator." In the pages of this lovely book, there are multiple instances of good teachers taking interests into account. They do so with a rare sense of the range of young people's concerns and, as well, a rare sense of the multiplicity of perspectives through which children can be helped to see the world as they learn and come to know.

Maureen Miletta opens a wealth of pedagogical possibility to her readers. She does so in part because she is speaking out of many years of lived experience with multiage elementary education, and in part because of her evident delight in discovering more and more things to explore and more and more modes of exploration. It is difficult to imagine a finer way of caring for children than by enabling them to expand their own horizons, to realize there is always something more to find out behind that tree, that rock, that wall.

This author and her colleagues have achieved this by (to use her language) "unbuckling" the traditional curriculum. To speak that way is to presume a constriction, a confinement where ordinary curricula are concerned. The approach described in this book is fundamentally metaphorical. During six- to eight-week "modules," children worked in groups on topics or problems they chose themselves: "My Robot Buddy," "Systems of the

Body," "Poetry Potpourri," "Mapping the USA," "Volcanoes and Earthquakes," and so on. More than what are ordinarily thought of as topics, they became (as it were) metaphors for expanding realms of subject matter with increasing relevance one for another.

As the book moves on, it becomes increasingly clear that Maureen and her colleagues made a deliberate effort to avoid ordinary categories and labels. Most of us are aware of how arbitrary grading by age has turned out to be, along with various "tracking" devices and traditional "grouping" techniques. In Maureen's classroom, every effort was made to recognize each individual child and to take his or her interests and predilections into account. As a result, children were far more likely to engage in the kinds of conversations that create communities. They exchanged ideas, took issue with one another, and tried to see through each other's eyes. In this fluid, variegated learning situation enriched by the presence of many books and other learning materials, the learning community formed and re-formed, in response to the children's interests and needs.

The teachers' flexibility of approach must be noted as well. At the start, for example, they offered students choices for mathematics just as they did for the other subject matter areas. After a number of years, however, they realized that the structure of mathematics and its dependence on sequence demanded another approach, so they thoughtfully considered the alternatives. What is presented here is in no degree an orthodoxy; the teachers involved are aware that there remains a range of options in every curricular field.

A Multiage Classroom is not a "how-to" book or a kind of lesson plan for would-be progressive teachers. It is, however, a storehouse of possible choices for teachers engaged in the creation of curricula and the development of a more reflective (and perhaps more enjoyable) practice. As such, it is implicitly a declaration of faith in teachers—most particularly in those who cherish their collaborative work with children and who nurture a love of knowledge, in whatever form it appears. There is no question but that the schools and pupils described in the pages that follow are privileged ones: the schoolrooms are well-equipped; there are fine library and laboratory resources; parents are available for help and support. In some respects, it may summon up for the reader the bleak and heart-tugging images in Jonathan Kozol's *Savage Inequalities* at moments of realizations that not many schools are like those presented in this book, nor can they be at this moment in our history. If we were *not* granted visions of realizable possibilities like the ones in this book, we would not be able to offer a significant response to Kozol, the kind of response that spells out what *ought* to be for every American child. In presenting possibilities for some of the open spaces in American public education as it exists today, Maureen Miletta offers perspectives—clear ones, exciting ones—on what a classroom ought to be for every living, growing young person. Her voice is eloquent and wise. In her very passion for learning and for children, she provides images of what Paulo Freire calls "a pedagogy of hope."

Maxine Greene
Teachers College, Columbia University

Introduction

Twenty-five years ago, Aileen Wissner, Esther Baranof, and I regrouped our fourth-, fifth-, and sixth-grade classes into a combined multiage classroom. We called it "The Interage Program," and it is still in existence today. This book recounts our efforts to create an atmosphere in which learning is valued, children have a voice in their education, and teachers have the freedom to create exciting, imaginative programs. It is my hope that our experience will prove helpful to other teachers who are interested in creating similar learning environments.

Today the talk of school renewal centers around many of the ideas that we incorporated into The Interage Program. Collegial decision making, thematic curriculum, inventive programming, community involvement, and the centrality of the arts were all part of our basic philosophy. They are highlighted in these pages, and I hope they may encourage others to initiate change within their schools.

It is important to point out that most of the book is written in the first person plural because we acted as a team at all times. If we wanted our students to become responsible decision makers in a supportive community, we knew that we had to demonstrate our own collaboration within the community we had created. We did that by avoiding the first person singular whenever we could. Students knew that we designed programs and decided issues jointly.

We recognize that we had the good fortune to be located in a suburb of New York City where we had resources not available to the majority of teachers. It might seem that it would be difficult to start an innovative program like ours without such an environment. But it wasn't our resources that motivated us—it was our desire to change the structure of the school and our belief that the classrooms did not have to remain as they were. We could imagine an ideal educational setting, and we thought that by designing and developing our own program we might influence other teachers to experiment with new ideas, new challenges. It can be done, even in an unsympathetic or indifferent environment, if you don't give in to cynicism and despair. Imagination fuels possibility, which generates persistence.

In creating our program, we knew we wanted to have our students with us for longer than usual. Many students don't begin to achieve success until the end of a school year, and we wanted to keep working with them as they continued to grow. Three years seemed ideal. We also felt that students would benefit from having more than one teacher available to them at all times. We designed our program for fourth, fifth, and sixth grades. But, in 1979, when the district moved all sixth graders into a middle school, we combined third, fourth, and fifth grades. Once the students entered our classrooms, however, they were never separated by grade level.

In many classrooms, then and now, there are stringent constraints placed upon the teachers, who not only need to "cover" subject matter for their grade but also must be careful not to trespass on the curriculum for the next grade. Schools have always compartmentalized learning into subject matter areas, and they have further limited it by prescribing exactly what one must learn in each grade! We relaxed those limitations, shuffled subject matter into exciting new (and not-so-new) patterns, and offered students the opportunity to choose what they wanted and needed to study. We certainly provided the full range of standard curriculum and paid careful attention to the development of basic skills, but we also were able to provide an impressive array of cross-disciplinary offerings.

We divided the school year into six-week "modules." This allowed us to change the subjects that the students could study every six weeks and to provide students with the chance for a new beginning six times a year instead of once. This notion of a fresh start, coupled with the idea of allowing students to choose their course of study from among a rich array of alternatives, gave The Interage Program its unique character.

In the eighteen years I was associated with The Interage Program, there were two years when only two teachers taught all three grades—both Aileen Wissner and I had sabbatical leaves to study at Columbia University. Also, since our retirement Barbara Sobolewski, who joined the team in 1973, has elected to work with only one other teacher, Elaine Sonnenberg, and the program has been changed to fourth- and fifth-grade. Barbara and Elaine work well together and decided not to risk the introduction of a new team member. The chemistry necessary to formulate a working relationship is essential.

In the following chapters I will recount a little personal history as well as the history of the program. I retired from the school system in 1989 to become a professor of education at Hofstra University, so I am looking back at the experience with the eyes of a teacher educator. I am still involved in a peripheral way, however, because I have been able to teach a topic during one or two modules a year. I continue to find it both challenging and rewarding.

The sections on curriculum are divided in traditional terms, even though we tried to stretch beyond the subject-matter boundaries whenever we could. In our classrooms, integration of subject matter never meant finding artificial correlations or connections for their own sake. Rather, those connections emerged as the result of intensive and in-depth study of a subject as students immersed themselves in meaningful and responsible investigations.

The final chapters deal with team-teaching, the creation of a democratic community, the involvement of parents, the assessment of our students, and the evaluation of The Interage Program by an outside team. These are important considerations for any teacher at any grade level in any community. We felt we were enormously successful in eliminating many of the problems that can arise. In many ways, we were pioneers.

Part 1

Filling in the Background

Chapter 1

Initiative and Possibility

At My Mother's Knee, 1940

I was desperate. In order to graduate from Kemble School and move into ninth grade at the high school, I had to complete a sewing project that I hated. Hated, obviously, because I was not adept at fashioning the tiny stitches. Hated, also, because the aptly named sewing teacher, Miss Crowe, kept reminding me of how talented my older sister had been.

I was not one to run to my mother or father with tales of school problems. Besides, I'd never seen my mother with a needle in her hand. I suspected she simply tossed out garments that needed mending. But desperation forced me to confess that Miss Crowe had threatened me with retention. My mother smiled her benevolent smile and fetched a needle and thread.

It was a freezing cold night. In upstate New York, winters were far more severe than any I have experienced in adulthood. Memory often exaggerates our perceptions, but I have clear images of snow piled up to the windowsills on the night my mother taught me to sew. We had an old stove which burned a coal fire. We often opened the oven door to enable the warmth to spread around the kitchen. On this particular night, we pulled our chairs up to its open door, moved a lamp closer, and propped our feet on the grates to toast our toes.

My mother then proceeded to demonstrate the most intricate stitching I had ever seen. She even taught me how to make buttonholes. And, as she stitched, she told me stories of her school in County Mayo. I thought she was the most talented mother and the best teacher in the world.

How did she know how to do all this? And why had I never seen her sew before? In Ireland, she had taught all the grades in a one-room schoolhouse at the foot of Crough Patrick, the mountain on which Saint Patrick was said to have driven the snakes from Ireland. Part of the curriculum for the girls—just the girls, mind you—was the making of a man's shirt. And my mother had taught them how to do it. She hadn't liked sewing and chose not to do it when she didn't have to, but she could do it. And that evening she gave me the skill and the permission to use it or to let it lie dormant until I needed it.

I loved her stories about teaching. She taught the "little ones" to read and even her rugged "big boys" to love the poetry of Shakespeare. She told stories of the sacrifices students made for studies and their privation for education. All of these became part of our family lore. From these stories, I must have absorbed something of my mother's style, my love of teaching, and my belief in its importance.

I tell this now, at the beginning, because in many ways I became my mother. I spent the last eighteen years of my elementary school career teaching in the modern equivalent of that one-room schoolhouse. In telling my story, I hope to be able to inspire others to find ways to develop their own personal style and to love teaching and learning as much as I have over a career that has lasted forty-four years and is still growing and changing.

Progressive Roots, 1950

I loved teaching from the first day I set foot in a second-grade classroom at the start of my career. Although I had originally wanted to teach English at the secondary level, I thought that with these young children I had found a place to put to use all that I had learned about music, art, history, science, math, and literature. Of course, it was only a few weeks before I recognized that what I'd learned wasn't enough. I found it so challenging to be with elementary school children that I realized I had to be a learner for the rest of my career.

Fortunately, that first year I worked as an assistant to a progressive educator with a talent for mentoring. We read and dramatized great children's literature from a collection of stories published in 1910. There were few pictures besides an occasional woodcut, but the children loved the stories. We wrote our own stories every day and collected them in classroom books. We kept animals in the classroom and studied their behavior— most memorably, two baby goats who lived in our bathroom for three weeks.

Sometimes we just sat in the large windows overlooking the busy East River and watched an incredible variety of boats go steaming by. The river was our backyard, our laboratory, and the key to unlocking our imaginations. But we didn't just observe the life of the city from our windows. We took trips all over New York. I loved to take the children to the Fulton Fish Market because the fishermen were all so impressed with their knowledge. The men would offer samples of every variety of seafaring creature imaginable and the children joyfully would carry them all home to their parents. I need not add, I am sure, that our odoriferous classroom bore the traces of our journey for many days thereafter.

Until that year, I hadn't realized what a challenge teaching young children could be and what fun it was to break down the artificial barriers of knowledge—to find ways to integrate learning through thematic units that cut across disciplines. From the day I started and throughout the next thirty-eight years of my life, I never again thought about teaching at a secondary school.

Closing the Gap, 1969

After teaching second grade for several years at the beginning of my career, I spent several more years teaching intermediate grades in a suburban public school. By 1969, I was beginning to wonder if I could still teach the younger classes and if I still had the resourcefulness, the stamina, to do it all again. When one of the second-grade teachers decided to retire, I asked if I might take her place. The principal favored teachers' changing grades frequently, so off I went to the other end of the building.

It wasn't easy to keep track of my former colleagues who taught sixth grade; I seldom saw them during the school day. I especially missed Aileen Wissner, with whom I had shared ideas and materials. We had also joined classes on many occasions for shared activities or units of study. We began to wonder if it would be possible to bring the second and sixth grades together.

To that end, we took both of our classes on a trip to an ice cream factory. One of the parents had volunteered to make all the arrangements because she did business with the factory. It was a memorable trip. The mother had told us it was less than an hour away, but it took us two hours to get there. Our hot, uncomfortable ride was only tempered by our visions of being greeted with triple-decker cones. Alas, they weren't expecting us! Put on the spot, the owners managed a tour of the premises and then tried to dish out small portions of ice cream from solidly frozen gallon packages to the salivating children. The adventure continued on the way home when we discovered that the brakes on the bus weren't working properly.

The trauma of the trip created a bond among us all, and from that day forth the sixth graders watched over their second-grade "buddies" with a diligence born of disaster. They often visited my classroom throughout each day to read stories, help with writing, or coach soccer games. I was grateful for the help and guidance they provided for my students, but it did not occur to me that this was a mutually beneficial arrangement until the day I observed two sixth graders playing with a group of younger children using Cuisenaire rods. All five students were interacting as equals and were deeply engrossed in the activity.

Aileen and I soon noticed this positive interaction and reinforcement of learning in other areas as well. The sixth graders had a new awareness of the importance of reading aloud and practiced stories they planned to share with their buddies. They were role models for the second graders, who began to ask if they might read to the kindergartners. As the older students helped with writing, their own writing and editing skills were sharpened. Most surprisingly, real friendships developed as mutual interests were shared.

Seeking Alternatives, 1970

By the following year, education was "opening up" all around us. Educators everywhere were being reminded that all children had abilities and that it was the teacher's job to find out what those abilities were and to develop them. In the past, self-contained classrooms too often locked children into predetermined categories and courses of study based on a definition of the "average" child. Now, teachers were being urged to match students' abilities and interests by grouping them without regard to age or grade. Based on our experience with the "buddies," we began to think that nongraded classrooms would make good sense. We read Goodlad and Anderson's *The Nongraded Elementary School*, which had been reissued in 1963. We knew from experience that what they said about graded classes made sense:

> In brief, . . . a fifth-grade teacher, in spite of his designation, is not a teacher of fifth-grade children. At a given time, he teaches third, fourth, fifth, sixth, seventh, eighth, and even ninth grades, as far as learner realities are concerned, even though all the pupils in his room may be labeled "fifth grade." Any attempt to deal with these children as fifth graders can only be Procrustean in its ultimate effects. (p. 3)

In the sixth grade, for example, there were students reading at a third-grade level as well as some reading at a high-school level. The same was true for math, and sometimes the students who were the mature readers were the ones having difficulty with math. We were constantly grouping and regrouping because these abilities were so diverse. And there was little time to pay attention to individual interests.

7

Aside from recognizing the impossible "Procrustean" task of teaching students at some fictitious grade level of competence, there were two main reasons that we were determined to create an environment free of ability grouping. First, we had seen enormous damage done to students who saw themselves placed on a continuum that categorized them as below average, average, or above average. Second, we found it difficult to truly individualize the curriculum when we were bound by what was and was not appropriate for a particular level.

Children labeled "below average" are often unhappy learners. Feelings of incompetence, frustration, and anxiety follow them throughout the school day. Even when given the opportunity to work individually with teachers trained to provide remediation, they know they are not working up to the level of their classmates, and their concentration is often shattered because they are worrying about their standing rather than focusing on the task at hand.

Similarly, no one likes to be just "average." The term implies mediocrity and the "average" children are apt to share some of the tension and frustration of those labeled "below average." Behaviorists tell us that this tension fosters competition and that the drive to be classified as "above average" is the incentive for success that we all need. We found, however, that the emphasis was always on the external quantification of success rather than on any growing awareness of the excitement of learning.

"Above average" students also seemed to focus on those quantifications. They were often preoccupied with the maintenance of their standing and were thus under considerable pressure to produce high-quality work. Too often the status produced an inflated sense of competence and an egocentric approach to knowledge.

We wanted to purposely enlarge the range of abilities valued so as to avoid categorizing students. In truth, any category system denies the individuality of children. Anyone who has ever taught would agree that the range of abilities, interests, and needs of children in any one classroom is infinite.

Learning styles also differ from child to child. Some students learn best when they study printed material; others must hear the spoken word. Some need to see a demonstration or to experience an activity firsthand. And some need a combination of media to fully comprehend an idea. Students should be exposed to a wide range of instructional strategies and should be able to move through the curriculum at their own pace.

We also saw a need to improve the climate of the classroom and the instructional setting. We thought some students would work well independently at times; others needed constant guidance and supervision. In our new classrooms, some could work in small groups, others in larger groups. We also believed that all our students would benefit from the presence of more than one teacher to whom they could go for instruction, advice, or consolation.

In addition, we wanted to create a different social atmosphere in school—one that reflected real life. If you watch the children of a particular neighborhood at play, you never see them make distinctions about age. As adults, we don't choose to socialize just with people of our own age. It seems absurd to even suggest it. Similarly, professional sports teams do not limit participation to one age group; veterans play side by side with rookies, and they learn from one another. In most schools, however, all the fifth graders play exclusively with other fifth graders on the playground. And you seldom see interage groupings encouraged for soccer or baseball. We hoped to provide our students with a more inclusive setting.

Taking the Plunge, 1971

One year later, Aileen's class and mine were still interacting in a positive fashion. There was a district-wide study group forming on the possibilities of alternative forms of schooling, and we were increasingly determined to underplay grade-level designations. We decided to pursue our goal further.

We were fortunate to have an innovative and collaborative principal, Margaret Dordick, who responded favorably whenever teachers came to her with ideas for change. When we met with Margaret, we discussed the fact that interage groupings were commonplace everywhere but in schools—so commonplace, in fact, that the idea of an ungraded classroom seemed a logical and natural extension of the way in which children interact in the real world. We had decided that we wanted a class that would not impose the traditional age divisions on our students. We also felt we needed more than just one year with our classes—three would be ideal. We hoped to eliminate that sense of frustration that all teachers feel when a year ends while they are just beginning to achieve success with students who need more time and only begin to blossom in the spring. Hearing our plans, Dr. Dordick was anxious to support us.

The majority of multiage classrooms we had been reading about were in the lower primary grades and had been modeled after the British Infant Schools. But we wanted to give parents a choice about placement, and there were not enough pupils at that age level in our school to incorporate them into a new program. It was a K–6 school, with a small K–3. Two other small K–3 schools sent their students for grades 4–6. Consequently, we had only one section for each of the primary grades, but four and five sections of fourth through sixth grade. In order to include a three-year span, our interage classroom would have to be a combination of fourth, fifth and sixth grades. We thought that Esther Baranof, a fifth-grade teacher, might be interested in joining us. (So often innovations take such an accidental but fortuitous turn—both the age group and the team of teachers were perfect combinations.) With Dr. Dordick's blessing, we started to plan for the new year immediately.

There is an important lesson to be learned from all this. One must never be afraid to take the initiative when possibilities present themselves. Too often, teachers wait to be told what to do. They rely on administrators, publishers, or education experts and authorities to tell them what should or should not be done in their classrooms. Teachers themselves must have the critical and creative capacities to make judgments and fashion innovative responses to educational currents.

The role of the administrator is crucial too. Margaret Dordick was the key player in helping us get this program off the ground. Her support, wisdom, and personal diplomacy were a constant source of inspiration. She was one of those rare educators whose own ego and career were always subordinate to her teachers. Her view of shared leadership and governance of schools was thirty years ahead of her time, and anyone who ever worked with her recognized the privilege they had been afforded.

Going Public, 1971

We were anxious to offer The Interage Program to parents as an option. Under Dr. Dordick's leadership, we developed a series of school-wide options that could be selected. Many teachers were anxious to have "open" classrooms. Others were ready to try team-teaching. The final placement of all children was left to the professional staff, but parents were encouraged to comment upon those organizational patterns in which they thought their children would grow best. We held an informal meeting for parents, and Dr. Dordick sent a letter to their homes. She outlined the possibilities and asked for a response. She also notified students of the multiple plans of organization and suggested that their parents might be talking to them about the options. Here is the text of her letter to students:

> Every year, teachers in our school work to study and discuss ideas that might improve our school. In the past, teachers have taken courses to learn about new social studies materials, to study how children learn, to study how to improve teaching and to learn more about many other areas.
>
> This year, teachers have been working on some ideas that they think will be interesting and helpful next year.

One idea is to have boys and girls of different ages working together in classrooms where there would be a lot of individual choices of materials and time to work.

Another idea is to have the social studies and science programs rely less on books and films or things inside the school and more on trips outside the school. For example, visiting the seashore, a clothing factory, or an art museum, or meeting with experts such as astronomers, sculptors, or physicians.

Another idea is to have two teachers work together or "team" for some parts of a curriculum so that one teacher who really loves mathematics can be the leader for that area while another who is a great writer can work with both groups for that. Still another idea is to have a special room as a laboratory or learning center with all kinds of ways to help figure out how to help individual children learn. This would include all kinds of books and materials, and all kinds of audiovisual equipment and materials.

While teachers still will decide where you will be placed next year, we have asked your parents to give us some advice in helping us make our decisions. Your parents have received information at meetings and in the mail. They probably will talk to you about these matters also.

What we hope to do is find a situation that will be just right for your happiness and growth.

The response to the proposal for The Interage Program was strong, and we were on our way.

We were housed in the old music room and an adjacent classroom. The music room was large—33' x 25'. Most fortunately, there was a large stage at one end. At the other end there were built-in cubbies. Since we planned to have no desks, these would serve as storage spaces for all the students. They were very deep and therefore spacious, although things at the back could easily be forgotten or overlooked. We once traced a putrid odor to find seven old lunch bags rotting in the back of one.

The area where instruments had been stored became our book closet, and we set about ordering multiple copies of good children's literature immediately. We moved our three teachers' desks together in an area and dubbed it the "office." Then we scavenged for furniture. We were able to find two large yellow tables that each could seat at least twelve children. We also acquired a number of cafeteria tables and chairs. We traded the children's old desks and obtained a number of round tables. We scattered bookcases around. Parents donated two beautiful couches, and a dentist who had just refurbished his office gave us his old furniture; it still sits in our classrooms today. We felt that it was important to create a relaxed atmosphere in the rooms. Since it would be necessary for the students to sit on the floor when we met with the entire group, the school district agreed to supply us with a large rug. The rug became a symbol of the sense of community that we wanted and were able to create.

I want to underline again that none of these arrangements were costly. We moved all the used furniture ourselves, and the money for multiple copies of books was money originally earmarked for textbooks. We simply substituted one for the other. Also, although we had two student teachers and an aide assigned to our team, their presence was not essential to the success of the program. There were many years when we had no such help, and the operation went just as smoothly.

I should also point out that there were a number of special area teachers, called "consultants," in the school. Industrial arts ("shop"), art, science, music, and physical education were all taught an average of once a week in special classrooms throughout the building. We integrated these services into our program, as well as those of a school psychologist and a school nurse.

So the stage was set to include multiage grouping and team-teaching. Students would spend three years in the program. Teachers would plan and work together and have the freedom to define their own roles. We hoped that a cohesive group would enable us to develop our own skills and knowledge as well as to form a support system as we tried new ideas and ventured into new curriculum areas.

For our students, we would provide a thematically organized, interdisciplinary curriculum affording them the opportunity to select areas of study based on their own needs and interests. As participants in the endeavor, they would design their own learning experiences. We would expose them to a rich curriculum in a stimulating and challenging environment. We hoped to foster intellectual purposefulness and the avoidance of busy work.

We knew we would have to look for new ways to "unbuckle the curriculum"—to think creatively about possibilities for integrating reading, writing, and social studies, math, and science. We looked for organizing concepts that would not only tap into the real interests of children but also use our own interests and capabilities to the maximum.

Chapter 2

A Community of Purposeful Learners

The First Days of School

Although no two school years are ever the same, the following description is typical of how we began each year. From the first day of school, students were required to make choices about what they would study. Since ours was a three-year program, two-thirds of our students were returning for either a second or a third year. First-year students met with the teachers for a short orientation while the others went to the gym. Upon their return, each new student was introduced by two buddies who had spent a few minutes getting to know her. If there were many new students, then we would devote a few minutes of each following day for introductions. We felt it was essential that all of the children know each other well, even when we had eighty.

We also spent about an hour on the first day of school talking about the philosophy of The Interage Program. It was important that all our students clearly understand not only the structure of the program but also the underlying assumptions we were making about teaching and learning. First, we asked them to think of situations outside of school in which they engaged in multiage activities. We wanted them to recognize that it is not unusual for mixed ages to work and play together and that developmental levels differed according to individual growth, not because they were ordained by grade level. We discussed the advantages of staying in the same classroom for three years with the same teachers, and we emphasized the value we placed on individual progress and cooperation, rather than competition. Team-teaching is a perfect illustration of this kind of cooperation, and we wanted our students to be aware that we were modeling the mixture of independence and interdependence that we hoped they would achieve.

The students talked about the excitement they felt at the beginning of each new school year, and we explained the organization of The Interage Program—specifically, the use of space and time. With our system of modules, students could look forward to flexible grouping and scheduling; they could experience the excitement of new beginnings every six weeks.

We spent the most time talking about informed choice and the making of decisions based on information and reflection. The first choice for the students to make concerned what kind of classroom environment they would like to create. On the first morning of classes, we began by discussing the importance of establishing expectations for the year and the need for classroom rules. As we prepared to formulate rules together, students were asked to initiate a discussion at home to determine what classroom rules their family members remembered from their school days. In this way we began to establish a connection between home and school life, and we signaled the importance of constant communication with parents.

Children came to school the following day with suggestions written in positive language—*dos* instead of *don'ts*. We condensed a long list on the blackboard and discussed and voted on each item before posting a final list of class rules on the bulletin board and stapling it into each student journal. Involving students in self-government helped shape a community of purposeful learners capable of assuming responsibility and handling the kind of freedom the program would allow. Each year the rules were worded differently, but the basic ideas seemed to remain. It is important to note that students must be given the responsibility *from the first day* to develop their own rules. Then, if there are infractions, they can be reminded of their participation in the creation of the governance. Teachers who fear giving over this responsibility will be assured by the degree of consonance between what rules they might have imposed and what students elect to live by. They will also be impressed with the self-discipline that results from the shared responsibility for the development of classroom democracy.

Here is a list that was developed by one year's class:

1. Be kind to your classmates and teachers.
2. Keep your hands to yourself.
3. Call people by their right name.
4. Please help as much as possible.
5. Return what you borrow.
6. Keep the noise level down.
7. Listen carefully.
8. Share with others.
9. Be civilized when working out a problem.
10. Walk in the building.
11. Raise your hand.
12. Tell the truth.
13. Be of good spirit.
14. Be a good sport.
15. Include others.
16. Obey our rules.

Too often, children only are given the opportunity to make choices that are really immaterial or irrelevant. On that first day we explained that in our classroom students would be making significant choices about what they wanted and needed to study. There would be the possibility to pursue special interests in great depth, and we hoped they eventually would want to teach others about those interests. We believed that when you learn to teach others, you learn how to teach yourself.

We wanted to be sure they understood that in order to have the right to make choices about their curriculum, they also had to accept the responsibility to pursue their studies purposefully. We also made it clear that we would be following the state curricular guidelines—we would study what other children their ages would study, but we would organize the studies differently. We would develop thematic units to incorporate and integrate the various disciplines.

To begin our program, we presented the students with a schedule of activities for the remainder of the week. Since school usually began two days after Labor Day, the schedule was usually for three days. Figure 2–1 represents one schedule of activities offered that first week.

While schedules were handed out and explained, newcomers to the group sat with their buddies, who provided assistance

	Wednesday	Thursday	Friday
9:30	Gym (returning students) Intro (new students)	Gym (returning students) Intro (new students)	Science (Greens) Art (Blues) Shop (Reds)
10:15	Large Group Meeting (LGM) (10:15–11:15)	First Group: Shop (10:15–11:15) Second Group: Log Entry (10:15–11:15)	Go over the schedule for First Module (10:15–12:00)
11:20	Groups: Science Fiction Newstime Science and Sports Pantomime Seascapes	Groups: Science Fiction Newstime Science and Sports Pantomime Seascapes	
12:00	Lunch	Lunch	Lunch
1:15	Logs	First Group: Log Entry (1:15–2:15) Second Group: Shop (1:15–2:15)	Reading/Logs
2:20	Groups: Shells Math Warm-Up Such Nonsense Word Games	Groups: Shells Math Warm-Up Such Nonsense Word Games	LGM

Figure 2–1

when needed. By this time they had already experienced the first two activities. Now it was time for the students to choose what they wanted to study. We explained each activity carefully so that the students could make informed decisions. Students who elected an activity knew what to expect and what was expected of them. We called the activity sections "groups," but perhaps they are best understood as "mini-courses."

After we briefly described each group, we designated a special area as the meeting place. The students were asked to go to their group's area immediately. Since we did not always have a separate room available for each group, it was almost always necessary to have two or three groups meet in one area. Instead of seeing this as a disadvantage, we focused on the necessity of respecting others' space and the need for quiet. The only time it became a problem was when the groups were involved in activities that generated energy and enthusiasm or necessitated noisy interaction of the participants.

On this day, the Science Fiction group was going to hear a short story by Ray Bradbury, *All Summer in a Day* (1959). They would discuss it and perhaps comment upon it in their journals. The Newstime group would discuss the main news events of the summer and present a report at the Friday Large Group Meeting (LGM). The Science and Sports group would investigate the newest theories about baseballs and their trajectories based on an article from *The New York Times*. Students choosing Pantomime would practice just that—they would work on skits based on well-known fairy tales. If our schedule allowed, they might present the skits to the entire class group at Friday's LGM. Finally, the Seascapes group would work on watercolors to decorate our empty bulletin boards. It was understood that all groups would meet again on Thursday, so the total preparation time for each activity was one hour and twenty minutes.

In the case of this particular schedule, we were able to offer five choices in this time slot. The three regular teachers taught three of the groups, a student teacher led the Science Fiction group, a fifth-grade student who had had experience organizing news groups offered the Newstime group.

After lunch, we devoted an hour to introducing the daily journals that the students would be required to keep. We called them "logs," and they became one of the most important components of the program (I discuss them at length in chapter 3). On this first day we talked about the importance of daily writing, the almost infinite choices that could be made about log entries, and the importance of the log as a record of their years in The Interage Program. Older students read stories, poems, reports, or reviews from their logs from previous years and shared tips with the newcomers about getting started. For the first entry we distributed a prompt, but students were not required to use it. We used a different prompt each year, but the questions were generally about how the students viewed themselves as learners and what they most enjoyed in school.

The last period of the day afforded another opportunity for choice making. We gathered again on the rug to explain the groups and where they would meet. This time the Shells group would investigate the classroom collection, sketching some and doing research on others. They planned to combine their work with that of the Seascapes group at the end of the week. The Math Warm-Up group would look at some difficult word problems and work at finding alternative solutions for them. The Such Nonsense group would read and write silly rhymes, and the Word Games group would play a variety of games such as Scrabble and Hangman.

The second day began much as the first. We reserved time to meet with the newcomers, and the older children went to the gym. Then we divided the entire class in two. Half of the class shared and discussed log entries in small groups. The other half went to the shop to learn how to use the machines. We repeated this arrangement in the afternoon, shifting the groups so that all had an opportunity to share logs, and all could go to the shop. The children also continued the group activities that they had chosen the previous day. By the end of this second day, the new students had a fairly good idea of how The Interage Program operated, and they were just as anxious as the older children for us to post the next week's schedule on Friday.

The First Module

We used the first period of each morning for our preparation period while the children participated in special activities with consultant teachers. When the students came back to class on that third day, they were greeted by a huge bulletin board filled with enticing signs announcing the new groups for the first module. We had stayed late the previous night to draw and paste these signs (many of which we recycled for years) to visually represent the choices and to underline the excitement we felt about the new offerings. Just as a book jacket invites the reader to further explore its contents, we wanted to entice our students to come to the LGM filled with questions about what the new offerings would include, what we would require of them, and what they might learn as a result of choosing each group.

Because the choices to be made involved a six-week commitment, it was important for students to listen carefully as each group was explained. We went over the content of each group and described the work required. When it was appropriate, we indicated the degree of difficulty.

The older students helped newcomers understand the scheduling process. They cautioned them to listen carefully to the descriptions and to be sure to include all subject matter areas in their schedules. They also gave short lectures on making intelligent choices, advising the younger students not to be influenced by what their friends were choosing. It always tickled us to hear these admonitions, particularly when they were delivered by those who hadn't always practiced what they preached. The counselors clearly felt obligated to set a good example for the advisees.

Picture if you can, a group of excited eight-, nine-, and ten-year-olds sitting on the floor and buzzing about what groups they wanted to choose. The excitement about subject matter and content was electrifying! Should they choose the group on Ancient Egypt or "Carmen San Diego?" Would *Tales of a Fourth Grade Nothing* (Blume 1972) be better than *The Lion, the Witch, and the Wardrobe* (Lewis 1950)? Did they need the group on numeration more than the one on exponents? Sometimes there would be forty children who wanted to join a particular group. In order to keep the size of the groups small, we would have to promise to offer it in the next module. We would take the names of the disappointed and promise them first choice in six weeks time.

All the groups were open to everyone, but there were some that demanded greater skill and knowledge than others, particularly in mathematics. Newer students, for example, didn't usually opt for algebra, although some third graders *were* ready for symbolic language and did successfully join advanced groups. That was the beauty of the design. We were really able to accommodate a vast array of capabilities and interests.

In most cases, however, the adjustment for age and experience was made as the children worked in the group. The teacher would guide each student toward an appropriate topic, study, or exploration within the group so that while they all were having a common instructional period, individual projects reflected individual aptitudes and attitudes. In a sense, that's not really very different from what a regular classroom teacher does every day. The difference here was that the children *chose* to study a topic and were relieved of the burden of group conformity. The limits were not defined by grade level but by each child's own interests.

Most groups met twice a week for forty or fifty minutes. The groups on Monday met once a week. Occasionally the selections were so enticing that students could not bear to miss a certain group and would end up with, say, three literature groups and no science. Schedules had to be approved by the teacher with whom the student conferred during a weekly conference. If we found that there was an imbalance in the choice of subject matter, changes might be negotiated or provision made for covering the material in the next module. The Appendix featured later in this book contains representative schedules that were developed for one academic year.

We also retained decision-making power by issuing "invitations" to children to join study groups that were designed to remedy certain gaps in learning. If we found, for example, that some students needed special help in reading strategies, place value, capitalization, or any number of hundreds of subskills in content areas, we would form a group to address those needs and ask certain students to join them. These were invitations that could not be refused. Interestingly enough, students never resisted joining them; our students actively sought help whenever they needed it and welcomed the opportunity to receive it in a regularly scheduled group. I think this was a by-product of the seriousness of purpose that developed because they were involved in selecting their curriculum. And since these particular groups were genuine thematic units of study, they were often chosen by other "uninvited" students who thought they sounded interesting.

There is an important point to be made here about the schedule. Because our school year was divided into modules of approximately six weeks time, the students were able to "begin school" six times a year. If they were unhappy or disappointed about their performance, they did not have to wait a year to turn over a new leaf and start again. The opportunity to reassess and reposition was afforded so often that students routinely performed self-evaluations and set new goals.

This was true for the teachers as well as the students. If we did not achieve all that we wanted during a particular module, we too could create a new page and take a fresh look at our teaching, our curriculum, and our goals. Although initially we had not envisioned this effect of the modular system, it became one of the greatest advantages of The Interage Program. We emphasized the significance of these new beginnings over and over again with students at the start of each new module and with parents during parent conferences.

Part 2

Making Curricular Connections

Chapter 3

Literacy and the Social Sciences

Reading was something we did all day long, and the study of social issues helped define our program. Both simply permeated the curriculum. When I look back at the group offerings of a particular year, I am hard pressed to define which are social studies and which are reading groups. There was time set aside after lunch for reading, but there was no subject ("group") specifically labeled *Reading* or *Social Studies*. Yet our students realized they were studying geography, history, or cultures and soon recognized that the primary way to gain information about their world and about themselves was through literature.

Materials

One way to understand the scope of these curricular studies may be to look at the materials that were available to both teachers and students. Students always had access to all the resources in the classroom and the school library. The importance of our collection cannot be underestimated—not only because of its quality and breadth, but also because of its availability.

Classroom Library

From the moment we started the program, we had control of our classroom's budget. Instead of ordering a basal reading series, we chose to buy multiple copies of trade books. Instead of purchasing social studies texts, we ordered beautiful books from the Smithsonian Institute, the Metropolitan Museum of Art, and the

National Geographic Society. These were all distributed on open shelves throughout the rooms and could be borrowed at any time.

We also collected shelves of paperback books donated by students, purchased at used book sales, and earned as bonuses from children's book subscription clubs such as The Trumpet Club and Scholastic Books. We had approximately eight hundred titles as a basic library, and we encouraged the children to add to it whenever they could. Parents also occasionally donated collections or purchased special volumes that they thought would be welcome additions. Often these donations came at the end of a year when a student would be leaving; the special gift would mark the "graduation" to the middle school. A "birthday book shelf" was also established, and the children and their parents usually donated a special volume to celebrate the occasion.

Special Subject Library

In addition to the general collection, we had special collections in "centers" throughout the classrooms. The section on social studies, for example, contained biographies of important historical figures, pictorial histories of events and periods, historical reference books, historical fiction, and some social studies textbooks useful for reference materials and background information.

In the science area we collected biographies and autobiographies of scientists, making sure to include as many women as possible. We also included information books about all the areas we covered in the curriculum, such as animals, the environment, magnetism and electricity, astronomy, and kitchen chemistry. These materials were available for reference work as well as for recreational reading during the day. We also had a section on health that contained all the material that we had accumulated about the human body. Children never stopped seeking information related to the systems and functions of the body.

Finally, we had a large collection of math books that were stored in a large walk-in closet devoted exclusively to mathematics. When we studied a particular concept, we selected the relevant books and displayed them along with the appropriate manipulative materials. Students read these books on their own and often became interested in teaching a math concept as a result of this recreational reading.

Professional Library

Two bookcases in our classrooms were devoted to books of primary interest to the teachers. Here were kept reference books for areas of specific study. These were also available to students who wished to explore advanced sources such as a collection of Matthew Brady's photographs of the Civil War or Pliny's account of the destruction of Pompeii. We kept a collection of folk tales from around the world here and an extensive collection of materials about race and gender equity. Because we were interested in the development of The National Writing Project, there were also many books about writing process.

Multiple Copies Library

We housed our most impressive collection of all in a giant closet originally used to store musical instruments. Here we kept multiple copies of the novels and nonfiction titles we used for group work. We generally bought twenty or twenty-five copies of each title, and over the years our collection grew to about two hundred titles. This "book room" was a favorite place for students and teachers, too. We loved to look at the vast array and never ceased to be tempted to spend an hour just looking over the specific titles grouped together. We were anxious to amass as many historical fiction titles as we could, believing that they provided a way to excite children about the study of history. For example, two shelves contained books about World War II and the Holocaust, including books about peace and nuclear warfare: *When Hitler Stole Pink Rabbit* (Kerr 1972), *The Upstairs Room* (Reiss 1972), and *Sadako and the Thousand Paper Cranes* (Coerr 1977).

We were especially anxious to teach American history through novels and biography in addition to information books. We collected books about the American Revolution, starting with the biographies of Jean Fritz, and books about the frontier, such as the Laura Ingalls Wilder series. In particular, children never tired of books about the Civil War period. We had multiple copies of *Harriet Tubman* (Petry 1955), *Frederick Douglass* (Patterson 1965), and *Jump Ship to Freedom* (Collier and Collier 1987).

Generally we grouped these books by theme. There was a shelf for immigrant studies, fairy tales, folklore, wildlife, the environment, and science fiction. If we accumulated a number of titles by the same author, we might group them for an author study. Realistic fiction was grouped by theme too. Novels about troubled children, independent girls, and bravery and courage were often grouped together.

We also kept a fine collection of poetry anthologies in this closet. Although we often offered study groups on poetry, we tried to use it across the curriculum as much as possible. The anthologies came in handy whenever we wanted to relate specific works to social studies.

At the end of every year when we would rearrange this huge closet, we often found new categories, discarded others, and generally determined which titles should be restocked and which no longer seemed as pertinent or as popular. If we found we had lost a large number of copies (some just "vanished"), we would move what remained into the classroom library where they could be circulated more readily. This was really a time for informally evaluating our reading program.

This spring cleaning occasioned much hilarity as we recalled incidents involving the children or colleagues or specific titles. We had ordered twenty-five copies of a book about pioneer life, for example, only to decide it was not suitable for our students. Those copies were moved from the section on the frontier to the section on courage to the section on women until finally we bundled them up and sent them to the middle school.

Often, in the midst of arranging and rearranging we would come upon a forgotten title or an old favorite that would stimulate our thinking about thematic units we might like to teach.

Charlotte's Web (White 1952) might become part of a unit on clever animals instead of a unit on rural life. Or we might decide to use it in a study of friendship.

Children loved to assist in this sorting and selecting. Often they had a better idea of where the books were located. Older students prided themselves on having read most of the titles, and we could hear them recommending good books to their younger classmates as they trained them to assume the responsibility for keeping the book room in order. The older students communicated their excitement about literature to the younger members of the group and perpetuated the literate environment we had originally established in the classroom.

There were often times when this sense of a "special space" helped us motivate reluctant readers. Students who were having difficulty finding good books to read felt privileged to be allowed to choose from among the multiple copies in the bookroom. We would often have a student–teacher conference here so we could pull out a number of recommended titles. We then would suggest that students read the first few pages of several novels to find at least one that would whet their appetite. We often would leave children sitting on a stool or on the floor surrounded with a collection of good books. In this way, they began to understand how to function in a library—a place that initially can be overwhelming to reluctant readers.

School Library

We were fortunate to have a well-stocked and well-run library in our school. Librarians play a crucial part in the development of literacy and are essential partners in the development of life-long readers and writers. Julia Sage, one of our librarians, taught me to ask a simple question when assisting children: "What was the last book you read that you loved?" That knowledge narrows the new recommendations and often helps pinpoint a perfect choice. Caroline Schwalbe Klimpl, another librarian, taught us how to listen carefully to children's responses in order to become thoroughly familiar with developing tastes. She not only knew every book in the school library, she also knew all the students well and was able to direct them to a variety of books with the secure knowledge that they would enjoy her suggestions. Under her direction, the library became an extension of the classroom, and we could send children there for weekly study groups. She would introduce new additions to the collection, teach library research skills, read aloud from well-loved picture books, or conduct ongoing author studies. The library was a showplace for dioramas, posters, and, most especially, the books written by the children. These were always added to the permanent collection for the remainder of the school year.

The Organization of Study Groups

Record Keeping

Many of our study groups had an emphasis on reading. Some were devoted to single titles—the students read and discussed one book. In others, students read a variety of titles as part of a thematic study. Some were specifically related to social studies or science. The poetry groups and writers workshop groups included both reading and writing.

We kept track of the reading groups that students selected so that we could discuss their progress at parent conferences or at conferences with the administration. Beginning in 1988, we used the computer to compile complete three-year profiles of our readers' habits. These profiles also included the scores on CTBS standardized tests and the scores on criteria-referenced tests given three times a year at the district's request. The district had adopted a reading program utilizing basal texts, and we were asked to demonstrate that our students were performing at least as well as their grade level counterparts. It is interesting to note that the tests were generally very easy for our students in spite of the fact that they had not read the basal texts.

We also kept a running record of the books our students read independently (see Figure 3–1). For each student, we divided a sheet of paper into ten sections and listed the books they com-

Independent Reading Record of _____	
Sept.	Oct.
Nov.	Dec.
Jan.	Feb.
March	April
May	June

Figure 3–1

pleted each month. A quick glance at this form, which we kept in the conference folder, would help us gauge the depth and breadth of a reader's choice and help us to guide future reading.

The Content of Study Groups: Literature

Each literature study group was different; the organization and the content depended, to a certain degree, on the children who had chosen that group. If a single title was used, we generally read the book together and discussed it. We often asked the children to think of three questions they would ask about a chapter. This was a great way to get them to think about the content. We taught them how to ask good, thoughtful questions instead of those that only necessitated a single factual response. It was always amazing to see how quickly they became expert questioners. This learning strategy is also an excellent assessment tool.

Often students wrote their questions in the same log they used to respond to the stories as they read them. Although the logs were never called "dialogue journals," they were often just that. If we wanted to emphasize the dialectical quality of reading, we responded directly in their logs so that a conversation between the teacher and the student might take place. (The children also responded in writing to each other.) Here, for example, is an exchange that occurred during the reading of *Shoeshine Girl* (Bulla 1975):

> *Student:* Ida is very mad at her parents because they sent her to her aunt's house. When I read about how sad and mad she was I felt very bad for her. But she doesn't seem like a very nice girl so far.
>
> *Teacher:* You're right—she is both sad and mad. Do you think she has a right to be sad and mad? What do you like about Sarah Ida?
>
> *Student:* I really don't blame Sarah Ida at all for being both mad and sad but since it is only for the summer I think she will get over it and things will get better.
>
> *Teacher:* We do get over things, don't we? "Time heals all wounds," we say.
>
> *Student:* Sarah Ida does not seem like such a nice person. She seems pretty obnoxious and selfish as well as unhappy. I think that it was very sneaky and greedy of Sarah to force Rossi to give her the money; she really didn't force Rossi to give her the money, but she knew that Rossi wanted very much for them to be friends. I wonder if Rossi will tell about the money and if Rossi and Sarah will become friends.
>
> *Teacher:* I wonder about that too. What leads you to think they might become friends?

This process helped our students to understand the transactional nature of reading and that even though our interpretations may differ, conversation about those differences can help us add to the meanings we uncover as we read. The accumulated meanings of the group added new dimensions to the literature; each book seemed to grow thicker as we discussed our reactions to it. As students read, we encouraged them to stop for a minute and discuss a controversial point with the person sitting next to them. Students often asked to pause for such a break because they had come upon something that surprised, amused, or outraged them. The new and the strange generally precipitated the most intense discussion. We hoped this kind of dialogue took place informally whenever students discussed the books they were reading.

Other skills, such as retelling a story or sequencing, could be emphasized by having the group dramatize the stories and present them to the entire class. These presentations at the LGM did a lot to stimulate interest in particular books, and there was always a demand for the titles after a performance.

For Halloween we often asked everyone to dress as a character in a book, and we would try to guess their identities by asking three questions. We also asked everyone to read a biography from time to time, and we would, again, ask the children to dress appropriately so their classmates could try to guess their identity. This kind of activity stimulates an interest in nonfiction and is particularly interesting when one particular subject matter field is chosen. For example, they might all be scientists, or mathematicians.

The Content of Study Groups: Social Studies

Most of the social studies units were thematic in nature. We wanted our students to love history and geography as much as we did. We all enjoyed regrouping our books in new ways and investigating issues that would help both students and teachers make new connections between the past and the present. We studied American and world history. We explored cultures and countries, civilizations and conflicts, often focusing on individuals who had had an impact on their time. We investigated discrimination, immigration, and environmental problems. We discussed the use of land, poverty, homelessness, diversity, and power. Students particularly enjoyed groups on the Civil War, the Revolutionary War, and ancient civilizations.

We had to repeat these topics often because of the interest they generated, but we would rename the group and shift the emphasis each time so that students could either begin or continue an in-depth study of the period. "The Civil War," for example, could become "Lincoln," "The Underground Railroad," or "Slavery." We could demonstrate that it was exciting to study a topic in depth, and we could emphasize the importance of specialized scholarly studies. Our students seldom complained that they had already studied a subject because they understood that knowledge is inexhaustible. We never heard, "Oh we had that last year," a common complaint in many classrooms. One student became an expert on the Civil War and years later returned from the high school to teach for us on his free afternoons.

We stressed the active involvement of students in social studies. Students were engaged in discussions, dramatizations, simulations, and constructions. They wrote personal narratives from the point of view of historical figures, dialogues between adversaries, news accounts, editorials, and historical journal entries. We held press conferences, news broadcasts, and panel discussions. We made matrices and Venn diagrams, wrote poetry, and drew political cartoons. We constructed maps and time lines and gave oral reports. In assessing the work, we asked our students what understandings had emerged from their studies and how they could demonstrate them. Because culminating activities were often shared with the entire class at LGM, they also served as a teaching and a motivating device for the students who had not participated in the particular unit of study. Through it all, we hoped that they would recognize that knowing how to learn and how to ask good questions was more important than knowing all the answers.

Whenever possible, we read primary sources. We used slave narratives and journals and read newspaper accounts of historical events. Students were particularly interested in Pliny's description of the destruction of Pompeii. Much of our work centered around biography. We also found Jackdaws, collections of primary source documents and photographs, to be useful even though they are designed for older grades. Hilda Taba had collaborated on a series of social studies texts for Addison-Wesley publishers that contained much primary source material and were useful in concept formation. The series was out of print but we salvaged enough copies to be able to use them with small groups.

We also took as many trips as we possibly could. During the first years of the program, our school building was in the heart of the downtown area, so we could easily walk to local sites. We visited bakeries, banks, art galleries, and studios. We sat on the floor of a leather shop and learned how to tool leather. When we later moved to a more suburban setting, we took as many bus trips as the budget would allow. We also visited homes in the area and talked with neighbors about everything from organic gardens to bread baking. We were primarily interested in helping our students understand how people live and work as individuals and in groups within our society.

Writing

When we started The Interage Program we wanted to make writing a central part of the curriculum, totally integrated with subjects ranging from social studies to art. We decided to require children to write every day. We didn't care what they wrote about, but we wanted to establish the habit of daily writing. From the beginning, we asked them to bring a black-and-white standard notebook to record SOMETHING at the end of every day.

We asked them to put the date at the top of each piece of writing, and we gave them suggestions for entries as needed. We might xerox a list of story prompts or post a few possible story titles. Sometimes we offered a study group called "Logs" that was specifically designed to stimulate ideas in smaller groups. These groups were especially effective for the younger children who had not had any experience with journals before entering The Interage Program.

Some students often wrote no more than one line a day. Many drew. Some made mazes. We accepted anything, read and reacted to the content in a conference, and set new goals for the next week. We hoped that the progress they were making would be readily apparent to the students as they looked back over their pages. Sometimes it was. Sometimes, however, it was embarrassing to see how little there was. In these cases, students often asked to literally turn over a new leaf, buy another notebook, and start all over again.

Our tolerance for these rough, beginning attempts at writing came from a profound belief that you learn by doing. In my own experiences as a student I had learned to love the cello because my teacher encouraged me to play in an orchestra almost as soon as I could draw the bow across the strings. I fooled around on the instrument a lot, but I learned discipline in that orchestra setting—and my playing rapidly improved. Sometimes parents and teachers alike have to have patience and realize that true understanding comes from experience.

Most children left The Interage Program with half a dozen books filled with recordings of their days in the program. Many left with ten. The children loved to read aloud from their logs at the LGM. And they also loved to listen to others read. This was a wonderful stimulus to writing. If someone wrote a wonderful science fiction story, we could count on several new variations in the next few days. And they learned from one another too. We watched the older children teach the younger ones all about baseball and football as they read their analyses of the week's games. Teachers also felt free to assign a piece of writing in the log for homework. They might request a first person narrative, for example, as homework from students studying a particular historical event.

We also used the logs in the study groups. At the beginning of a lesson we would ask our students to write down what they thought they were going to learn. At the conclusion of the lesson we would ask them what they thought they had in fact learned. This would constitute the entry for the day unless the students had more to add when they got home.

What was most exciting for the teachers was to see the growth over time that the logs represented. After three years, writing a daily journal became a habit for some and an outlet for others. Many of our students continued to keep a journal after leaving The Interage Program.

Effective as the logs were, however, they did not represent the whole of the writing experiences. In each of the study groups there was always an emphasis on various types of writing. Students wrote letters to authors, newspapers, parents, and politicians. They wrote brochures, pamphlets, and articles. Most often these pieces were not assigned but rather grew out of the children's own interests, inquiries, and impulses.

Marcia, a former student who is now a high-school senior, worked at the municipal swimming pool where I did my daily laps last summer. I didn't recognize her at first because I hadn't seen her in over six years. The changes that take place between ages ten and seventeen are profound! One morning, Marcia stopped me. "I just wanted you to know that I plan to be a writer," she said. She was looking at colleges and was paying particular attention to English departments. She felt that the start she'd had in The Interage Program had been influential in developing her ability and her love for writing. She lamented the fact that subsequent school years had not provided her equivalent opportunities, although she'd been active on the school newspaper.

We spent about half an hour reminiscing about her years in the program. Marcia said she had saved almost all of her writing. One day, she brought me a shopping bag full of her journals, and I spent a pleasant evening rereading the notebooks she'd filled during her three years with us. In her final year-end evaluation she wrote, "One of the best things about the Interage is how you write a log. You get to write stories, poems, and to express your thoughts on paper. It also improves your writing. I love writing in my log. My writing skills have improved dramatically."

It was obvious that Marcia's writing had improved. This growth-over-time quality of the journals was one of the most effective ways to demonstrate achievement to parents. But equally interesting was the diversity of her writing. When parents read through a child's entries, they receive a clear picture of what is happening in the classroom. The log becomes a source of communication between the school and the home. Here, for example, are some of the things Marcia wrote. The first was an early entry when she was a third grader:

What I Would Like to be Like

Wherever I go people say I have beutifull hair but they never say I have beutifull eyes. I either want green eyes or blue eyes.

I hate the people who eat alot and never get fat. I can't do that. I wish I could.

I want to be smart but not a nerd. I have a normel brain.

As a fifth grader she wrote lots of poetry:

Marbles

I watch
as the
smooth
glass
marbles
roll
across
the floor
Hitting
one another
Forcing them
to move on
Until
the distance
that
they move
gets smaller
and smaller
and then
they
Stop.

Marcia also wrote ABC books and pop-up books. Often she wrote about the books she was reading. She commented upon the groups that she was in and frequently wrote first person narratives about the lives of people she was learning about. There were stories of slaves, explorers, Florence Nightingale, Ivan the Terrible, Betsy Ross, and Benjamin Franklin. She continued to write self-evaluative pieces. Here's one from June of her fourth grade year:

What I Learned This past Year

I've learned how to be a better friend. To say. "I'm sorry" even though I didn't do anything. I learned not to let people boss me around, to set a good example and to do what *I* think is right. I learned not to let my social life interfere with my school life. I've done all the things that I wanted to achieve higher in such as, spelling, reading, math, history, writing and athletics. We've seen and learned a lot from all the productions we've seen. We had a great experience from doing the pirates of penzence. I've helped a lot of younger kids and sometimes older kids. From the first day to the last I've tried to help. I've recommended books to people, showed them where things are, helped them with homework and more. I think I've done my share as a fourth grader in the Interage and I'm ready to face being a fifth grader in the Interage.

There has been a shift in the emphasis since third grade, when Marcia told us she wanted green eyes. In her self-evaluation this year, she enumerates the ways she's helped others and announces that she's met her academic as well as her social goals. She's also better able to articulate what she's experiencing. Here are two other entries from that year:

The Chinese New Year

Today in school Mrs. Lee, Billy's mom came in to talk about the Chinese New Year. First she gave us a sheet with the Chinese zodiac. "It is the year of the dragon," she said. The dragon is special. It is the only animal out of all the zodiac signs that doesn't exist. The reason why the cat is not a zodiac sign is because the rat told the cat there was a party on Sunday but it was really on Saturday. The king was putting the animals on zodiac signs and the cat missed it. The zodiac signs are Rat, Ox, Tiger, Rabbit, Dragon, Boar, Dog, Snake, Cock, Monkey, Sheep, Horse. I'm a horse. They make lots of paper cats in China. The adults give children little bags with Chinese designs on them. If you get pennies in them it's good luck.

Our Class Play

This year of 1988 my class the Interage performed a great play production of "The Pirates of Penzance" written by Gilbert and Sullivan. It was one of the best experiences of my life. I think we did great. We cooperated and no one complained or bragged about their part. I wasn't nervous until the night performance. I started laughing in the middle of the song climbing over rocky mountain. I was so nervous. This kindergarten kid came up to me and said "I loved your play." I felt really good when people said how good it was. There were at least 20 people video taping the show and at least 100 people taking pictures with flashes going off every 2 seconds. The party afterwards was nice. You got to talk to people about the play and more pictures. The teachers said it was the best play we ever did. Like every year. The worst thing about the play is that it's over. I'll miss it.

Marcia reminded me that I'd encouraged her to be a writer. I hadn't remembered, but she knew exactly what had impressed her. She recounted in great detail a story she'd written called "Oops!" about a sudden error in judgment she'd made. I had apparently urged her to write a series of "Oops!" stories, and when I asked her to copy them from her log and make a cover, she was pleased. "Honored," she said, remembering. The book was displayed at Open House, and Marcia was so excited that she decided to become a writer.

As I listened to Marcia, I was reminded that teachers profoundly affect the lives of their students in little unremembered acts of faith and inspiration. Encouraging her and displaying her book was routine for me, but it had a dramatic impact on Marcia.

Chapter 4

Science and Mathematics

Making Science Meaningful

In many ways it is easiest to integrate science into a multiage program. Because of its investigative nature rooted in experimental, "hands-on" exploration, there is a lot of room for individualization. At the same time, science lends itself to collaborative problem solving in flexible, task-oriented, heterogenous groups.

Children are naturally curious about themselves and their world. They want accurate and relevant information about the complexity of plants and animals. Helping them organize approaches to obtaining this information can model a more general approach to inquiry, analysis and decision making. And because there are fewer pressures on children to get the "right answer," inquiry in science looks more freely at hypotheses, multiple meanings, and possibility.

As teachers we may have also felt more involved in the pursuit of understanding. Perhaps this is because scientific thinking is front page news these days as we push open new frontiers in technology. Since we always felt we had as much to learn as the children, we took on co-learner roles. We were as eager as our students to see what new developments would headline the science section of *The New York Times*.

Methods and Materials

As always, we amassed a great collection of materials and books for our classroom library. We were fortunate to have a science "consultant," a special teacher in each of the district's elementary schools. These consultants not only taught science classes but also provided the classroom teacher with ideas and materials. In addition, they outfitted their own classrooms as laboratories where students could interact with animals and conduct experiments with the equipment. Students also knew that they could bring in any "treasures" that they had discovered if they needed help with identification from an expert.

Of course, we had animals in our classrooms as well. Their care and feeding were an integral part of our studies, and children made careful observations of their behavior and charted their growth. We had snakes that presented us with offspring as well as rabbits who produced seven bunnies for us. Aileen's husband, Irwin, taught in a school in New York City that had an agriculture department. Irwin's school raised chickens, and one day someone left a young hen on their doorstep. Fearing it would not be accepted by the other chickens, Irwin brought it home to Aileen who promptly brought it to school. The children named her Henrietta and lavished on her the same tender care with which they raised all our animals. Henrietta thrived and began to crow in happiness every morning—at which point we realized we'd made a slight mistake of identity. Henrietta was renamed Henry, spent a peaceful few months with us, and was then retired to a children's petting farm.

Most of the animals were kept in the lab, however, where they could be "borrowed" for a weekend or a vacation to give all children the opportunity to care for a pet at home. The presence of these animals in the science room helped make it a focal point for students before and after school.

In addition to supervising the laboratory, the science consultants wrote guides for each classroom teacher. Focusing on specific areas of study such as magnetism or machines, each guide contained a list of basic principles and a sequence of generalizations followed by a series of activities with simple illustrations. The guides also contained a glossary and a bibliography of teacher resources and children's books. They were exemplary, and we all learned to teach science from them.

When we started out, we also used many of the materials published in the sixties when the reform movement for the teaching of science and mathematics was at its height. We were involved in the Conceptually Oriented Program for Elementary Science (COPES) because our science consultant, Al Hertzberg, had been a member of the New York University team that authored it. We also used the materials that Al helped develop on teaching principles of astronomy to elementary school children.

The Education Development Center (EDC) at Newton, Massachusetts, sponsored a project called "The Elementary Science Study" (ESS). This project offered kits containing units on "Gases and Airs," "Small Things," "Kitchen Physics," "The Behavior of Mealworms" and "Growing Seeds." These were extremely useful to us because we could build a unit around the topic of the kit and insert it right into our program. Students were allowed a good deal of autonomy in working with the materials, which led to individual observations and hypotheses.

More recently we have used the materials developed by the Activities Integrating Math and Science Educational Foundation (AIMS). But, as with all commercially packaged materials, one must use caution. There are a lot of dittos accompanying the AIMS materials, and they must be used judiciously lest the emphasis shift away from inquiry and process.

Curricular Choices

There was agreement in our school that all fourth grades would study plant and animal life, geology, and weather; fifth grades would study the human body, electricity, and simple machines; sixth grades would study astronomy, chemistry, and microscopic life. These three areas represented the minimal focus for the year. We studied them all and many more.

In the first half of one year, we had groups on the following topics:

Killer Storms. We investigated hurricanes and tornados.
Growing Things. We tested the requirements for seeds to germinate and grew vegetables from cuttings.

Microscopic Water Life. We collected water samples from fresh and salt water and compared the two.

Sea Monsters. We researched the legends of sea monsters and searched for explanations.

Science of the Week. We conducted a different experiment or demonstration each week.

Ashokan. We helped prepare our older students for a week of nature and archeological studies at a woodland campsite.

The Pollution of the Environment. We focused on active ways of preventing pollution.

Sharks and Whales. We visited an aquarium after doing research and sharing our findings at the LGM.

Evolution. We focused our studies on Leakey.

Science You Can Eat. We used a book of the same name by Vicki Cobb (1972).

Let's Find Out. We did individual research projects based on the questions that group members had. Bulb and battery question-and-answer boards were constructed in the shop.

The World of Animals. We made habitats in shoe boxes. The culminating activity was a trip to the Bronx Zoo.

Astronomy. We began with Archimedes's proof that the world was round and ended with the current space explorations.

Dolphins. We compared fiction and nonfiction accounts of dolphins.

Microscopes. We borrowed individual microscopes from the science lab, looked at living things, and sketched them in our science notebooks. We also visited the laboratory at the high school.

Women and Men in Science. We emphasized and demonstrated that science is not just for the boys. We made Rube Goldberg-type inventions.

Nutrition. We focused on healthy eating with lots of in-class cooking.

Here's another list from a different half year that demonstrates both the range of offerings and the repetition of basic concepts. "Pollution of the Environment" has become "Rachel Carson," and "Growing Things" has become "Oats, Peas, Beans," for example.

Flowers
Environmental Safari
Rachel Carson
Pendulums
Our Solar System
Seashore Ecology
Experimenting With Science
Fishes
The Eye
Liquid Magic
Plenty of plants
Oats, Peas, Beans
Simple Machines
The Age of Dinosaurs
Photography
The Invisible World
Forces in Nature
The Human Body
Science of the Week
Atoms and Molecules

There is nothing in these lists that is not studied in regular elementary classrooms. The difference is that the children were free to choose what they were interested in studying, were free to choose the subcategories that they would research, and were able to work in heterogenous groups composed of children from three traditional grade levels. Relationships were not based on age, gender, status, or ability level. The emphasis was on problem solving through hands-on, concrete experiences that would help formulate conceptual understanding.

Making Math Meaningful

Our goal was to make math instruction in The Interage Program inquiry-based, recursive, collaborative, and thematic. We wanted our students to love math, so we set about to make them feel capable and confident in their own ability to manipulate numbers and to reason mathematically.

In the first years of the program, we allowed the same student choices for math as we offered in other subject matter areas. But the structure of the discipline kept reminding us that it was more linear and more sequential than others. We never felt as comfortable allowing our students to freely select their math groups. Or perhaps we hesitated to trust ourselves to teach the diversified groups that such openness would bring. I think we also had more worries about the standardized tests that our students had to take every spring. They required competence in computation, for example, and we did not want to place our students at a disadvantage because we had not stressed an algorithm that they would encounter on the tests.

In any event we wavered on math, and after about ten years of complete choice, we began to limit it. We finally abandoned multiage grouping in math for most of each year. We had discovered CSMP, the Comprehensive School Mathematics Program, and after experimenting with it for a year or two we decided to adopt it for all our students. Because it was graded material, we divided into grade level groupings for math instruction four times a week. There were a few exceptions to the grade level groups, but for the most part we each taught either third, fourth, or fifth graders.

Interestingly enough, no one objected. The work was stimulating and the materials sufficiently innovative to capture everyone's enthusiasm. In addition to developing knowledge of number systems and competence in operations with numbers, CSMP includes an early introduction to integers, rational numbers, and decimals. Geometry and measurement, as well as probability and statistics, are not treated as separate areas but are included throughout the studies.

We felt that the materials of CSMP furthered our own goal of building our students confidence in their mathematical abilities while strengthening their love of math activities. One other advantage was the spiraling nature of the program. A variety of experiences are provided and topics are repeated through increased levels of difficulty. As the experiences recur, learnings accumulate and offer opportunities for the formation of ideas and the solutions of problems.

We supplemented the program where we deemed it necessary and continued to offer math enrichment in the full schedule. Was it ideal? Probably not. At this writing, Barbara and Elaine have abandoned CSMP but continue to instruct their fourth and fifth graders in grade level groups. They have also added certain enrichment topics that can be chosen by all. They are considering enlarging the number of choices and cutting back on the grade level groups as much as possible.

Errors and Expectations

When we were students in elementary school, we had been taught to think of math as the determination of right and wrong answers and the ability to compute accurately and quickly. Rules were to be remembered and applied, and the textbook represented the final authority. When we became teachers, we tended to teach as we had been taught, but with the advent of the "new math" in the sixties, we began to think of math as exploration and discovery. Many of us who had considered ourselves informed teachers of mathematics learned to reexamine and reanalyze our conceptions and misconceptions about mathematics teaching.

This examination led, logically, to helping our students explore their assumptions about mathematics. The emphasis shifted from right or wrong answers to an analysis of the processes students used to arrive at their answers.

What we discovered was that so-called "careless work" was often evidence of elaborate mental activity and that students' unique solutions to problems frequently involved highly logical and efficient methodology. In all our math groups, strategies for problem solving and the logic of an answer were emphasized in new ways without sacrificing the rigor and exactitude we had helped our students to value.

We also made certain that the girls saw themselves as capable in both math and science. From the beginning we focused on the equitable treatment of boys and girls, and we emphasized in all our groups that opportunity for advanced study in mathematics was available for both sexes. Our expectation that girls could and should do all that the boys did was part and parcel of the educational climate that fostered the kind of growth we deemed essential.

Methods and Materials

When we began our program we collected math materials with the same fervor that we acquired books. We combed catalogs for interesting manipulatives and over the years ordered almost everything that was available from Creative Publications and the Cuisenaire catalog. We housed these materials in a closet that had been used to store musical instruments. There were counters of all sizes and shapes, ranging from an impressive collection of beach stones to old wooden poker chips. There are boxes of dice and spinners, tangrams and pentominos, Dienes blocks, geoboards, Cuisenaire rods and Napier rods, pattern blocks and People Pieces, clocks of all sizes, calculators, road maps, number lines, geometric shapes and solids, scales, compasses, protractors, rulers, fractional parts, measuring devices for both English standard and metric systems, symmetry mirrors, wall charts, posters, and every conceivable game to reinforce math concepts.

If you are already asking where we obtained the funding for such an array of math materials, remember that we did not order any math textbooks. That meant we could use the money to purchase meaningful materials. Since we planned to allow our students to control and manipulate much of their own mathematical learning, we wanted to have materials available that were as diverse, novel, and complex as possible.

Even without funds, however, most of the materials mentioned can be fashioned from materials that can be donated or brought from home. Having children make their own manipulatives was also an effective teaching device.

In addition, we ordered many teacher resource books and pamphlets. We wanted to be sure that we had an abundance of reference books on all mathematical topics. We loved Marilyn Burns's *I Hate Mathematics!* (1977), for example, and the materials from Project AIMS. Ideas and activities that seemed to us most suitable for the instructional task and the individual child were culled from each source. We also purchased one copy of several textbooks so that we might use them as references.

As we planned the curriculum for each module, we tried to offer as many conceptual areas as possible. We often began by focusing on numeration and place value, estimation, mental computation, and the algorithms associated with addition, subtraction, multiplication, and division. We wanted problem solving to be at the center of our students' mathematical reasoning no matter what area we were concentrating on. After the first module we began to offer fractions and decimals, geometry, probability, and statistics. As always, we subdivided these topics and often gave them inviting names in order to identify content and attract attention.

Here is a list of the groups offered in the first half of one year:

Module 1

Metric Mania
Attributes
Palatable Plotting
Clock Arithmetic
Problem-Solving
Metric City
Beginning Graphing
Decimals
Multiplication and Division
Division Review
Zero to Zillions
Math Lab

Module 2

Algebra
Division
Number Theory
Word Problems
Algebraic Formulas
Figure Replication
Operations
Metric Review
Beginning Fractions
Geoboards
Fractions
Percentage
Multiplication and Division
Supercube Math
Math Lab

Module 3

Geometry
Problem Solving
Other Bases
Long Division
Math Workshop
Madison Project
Fractions
Operations with Fractions
Probability
Decimals and Percentage
Money
Math Lab

It is apparent that almost all areas of the math curriculum were offered as choices in each module. The difference was that students did not have to take them in sequential order. They could choose geometry without feeling completely secure with the division algorithm, for example, because there was an expectation that they would return to division in an upcoming module.

This flexibility made an enormous difference in the way in which students viewed themselves and their mathematical capabilities. Alicia, for example, had been in the lowest reading and math groups in her second-grade classroom. When she came to us she was quiet and shy, preferring to let others do most of the talking at LGM. I was teaching a beginning geometry group that Alicia joined. I introduced Venn diagrams and the sorting of geometric shapes according to three attributes: size, shape, and color. There were two sizes: large and small; three shapes: circles, squares, and triangles; and four colors: red, green, yellow, and blue. There were twenty-four pieces in all. We played a concept attainment game that involved having teams of students test hypotheses about how the circles of the Venn diagrams had been labeled.

Alicia loved this game. She seemed to grasp the categories faster than anyone else, and she seldom placed a shape in the wrong position in the diagram. Her classmates were surprised at first and even remarked on the fact that she had been in the "lowest" math group in second grade. They quickly recognized her ability, however, and were outwardly happy when she ended up on their team. She would walk to the blackboard with great self-assurance, beam from ear to ear when told that she had guessed correctly, and return to her seat with a little skip accompanied by a low hiss of "Yesss!" from her team. By the end of the module Alicia saw herself as a capable math student, was ready to tackle computation again, and was the close friend of one of the most sought-after girls in the class.

Another advantage of allowing children to choose what most interests them is that their motivation is so great that they are always attentive in class and eager to learn new concepts. I recently completed a unit on algebra with the fourth and fifth graders in the present Interage Program. I met with them once a week during a spring module, and because we hadn't finished all the work we had intended to do, we extended the group for a second module. I worked with fourteen students, equal numbers of boys and girls and fourth and fifth graders. I was not well acquainted with these children and did not know their ages or anything about their academic achievement. Working with the group, I was unable to distinguish the grade level of any child. Nor was there any difference in the participation, the method of inquiry, or the level of thinking in the boys and the girls. What most impressed me was the desire they all had to understand and learn from the mistakes they made and to help one another to analyze the work.

Parents As Part of the Process

It was also important to help parents to understand how children's mathematical thinking develops and to enlist their support in furthering our objectives at home. Problem solving requires imagination and the ability to mentally recreate a situation. Conceptual understanding does not come automatically with exposure to manipulatives. It is an ability that must be nurtured through increasingly sophisticated levels of experience both in and out of school so that students can realize the satisfaction and the joy of achievement.

Parents should be warned against sharing with their children their own possible hostility to mathematics. It can offer students justification for failure if they learn that their parents hated or performed poorly in math. We also cautioned parents about false dichotomies between the new and the old techniques or how they were taught and how math is taught today, between skills and concepts, between concrete and abstract thinking, and between structure and problem-solving approaches. We explained that we always try to achieve a balance between teaching skills and concepts or between concrete or abstract reasoning. Math is too important to become the target of warring schools of thought.

We also cautioned parents against purchasing workbooks that were only drill reinforcement for children. Instead, we offered suggestions for interesting activities that could be undertaken at home, would strengthen math concepts, and would provide ways of obtaining competence in computation without the use of flashcards.

We shared with parents the strategies we taught students to use when solving problems: experimenting; making charts, maps, pictures or diagrams; looking for patterns or similar problems; working backwards; trying to simplify; and using equations. During parent meetings we would discuss the importance of estimation in mathematics, or we would model activities suitable for the home. We suggested that parents help their children make scale drawings of the house, or bar graphs of grocery costs or the differences between heating costs throughout the year. We helped parents to understand the importance of process and urged them to ask questions of their children rather than telling them how to solve problems. Most of all, we emphasized that mathematics is stimulating, enjoyable, and capable of bringing great wonder, joy, and beauty into their children's lives.

Chapter 5

The Arts

Part of the Routine

Looking outside the classroom window, I could see the clouds rising from the horizon. Huge, black, menacing shapes tumbled across the sky, promising a deluge. We had been discussing the equitable use of technological equipment, but I stopped the discussion, switched off the lights, and asked the class to gather around the twelve-foot arched windows that stretched across one wall. The windows were the perfect frames for the drama unfolding in the sky. We noticed the incredible elasticity of the trees as they were caught by the wind. We identified cloud types and, as the room darkened, we discussed how an artist might capture their colors and shapes. Most important we discovered that the sky, which was usually just background, played the central part in the picture developing before our eyes. We must have watched the approaching storm for almost half an hour—sometimes in silence, sometimes sharing insights or stories.

You might question why I interrupted the flow of instruction to watch the approaching storm. But it was routine. Unanticipated events often offer significant teaching opportunities, particularly in the aesthetic realm. Developing students' aesthetic awareness was an important curricular goal and, I wanted my students to be as attuned to natural events—and how they might capture them in words or in pictures—as they were to the latest news report or the formula for the circumference of a circle.

The children in that group never filled in the background of their paintings with blue tempera again. I like to think that they never stopped looking at the infinite cloud combinations or colors of the sky, just as I like to think they will never stop marvelling at the formula for the circumference of a circle.

We wanted our students to become lifelong learners, paying careful attention to their world, making entries in their journals and noting images in their minds. There is always more to learn, and the more we learn, the more we want to learn. There is always more to see, and the more we see, the more we want to see. The arts keep us looking, feeling, and thinking. Here are some of the ways in which the arts were integrated into every aspect of The Interage Program.

Purposeful Activity

On a typical spring afternoon, this is what one might have found in our classroom. On the large pink rug a group of children were painting part of the scenery for "The Mikado," an upcoming production. At one end of the room on the raised platform that constituted a stage, Jamie, Susan, and Michael were fashioning choreography to go with their song, and Matt and Carol were composing lines that could be added to the script so that more students could have at least one line of dialogue.

A five-foot bulletin board stretched across the length of the back wall. Here we collected, in more or less chronological order, all kinds of art reproductions representing most periods in art history. Postcards and posters displayed a range from Lascaux cave drawings to Schnabel and Stella. Two students, Clinton and James, were looking for examples of perspective to help them with a sketch of a pyramid.

All the walls were covered with drawings. paintings, and books made by the students. Some drawings were based on the study of ancient civilizations—they included hieroglyphs and dark-eyed pharaohs. Geometric patterns painted in math class were displayed next to detailed drawings of forsythia, just completed by a nature study group.

The purposeful activity engaged all of the children and it

would have been difficult at first to locate the teachers among the students. In fact, there were parents there too, donating their time to help with the Gilbert and Sullivan production as well as sharing their own creative efforts. Ira's mother had recently begun to write for the local newspaper and planned to read two short stories she had just finished. She would solicit feedback from the students and share with them some of the joys and agonies of writing. Writers, as well as painters, musicians, dancers, and dramatists open imaginative worlds to us and keep us from being swallowed up by the daily exigencies.

The current schedule also included a course on aviation taught by the principal, who was anxious to be a part of the team as often as time permitted. The photography group was taking pictures of neighborhood houses and identifying architectural styles. The Old New York group was working on models of New York City in the early part of the nineteenth century. The Ancient Civilizations students were painting large murals based on Etruscan tomb paintings.

We wove literature into all the curricular groups, several of which had been organized around specific titles. As the children who were reading *Charlotte's Web* (White 1952) or *Ben and Me* (Lawson 1951) met in their groups, they responded to the aesthetic elements in the story, visualizing scenes, exploring characterization, finding relevance, and analyzing metaphorical language. They responded to their reading in their logs, which then became an ongoing record of their discussions and explorations.

All sixty-eight students prepared for the production of "The Mikado." We had chosen three Gilbert and Sullivan operettas that seemed particularly suitable for the elementary school—"Pirates of Penzance," "The Mikado," and "HMS Pinafore"—and we alternated them each year so that our students performed in all three over their stay in The Interage Program. Gilbert and Sullivan operettas were perfect because there was no limit to the number of pirates, maidens, sailors, or gentlemen of Japan that we could put on stage. There was an added bonus in terms of vocabulary development because the dialogue was so rich. The students were involved with every aspect of the production. They learned all the music and the dances. They designed and painted scenery. They helped assemble costumes. It was a group effort in every way and the final evening performance was always a triumph. What made it most exciting for the teachers and parents was that new talents were always uncovered; the participation in such an artistic endeavor revealed hidden propensities and possibilities.

Picasso and Velázquez

In one particular module we scheduled a mini-course called "Famous Painters" in which we consciously set out to study and then reproduce some of the world's masterpieces. I had seen an exhibition of children's pictures in San Sepolcro, Italy, in which students had copied the work of Piero Della Francesca. They first had to understand the geometric proportions in his paintings and then create three-dimensional reproductions using collage techniques. We tried to do the same, seeking primarily to become familiar with the artists and their work. By using a grid, some students made quite literal copies of the paintings. Others captured the colors or the shapes of a particular artist whose work interested them. When the module ended, students asked if we could study Picasso more intensively because they had enjoyed his paintings. As a result, we scheduled a group called "Picasso" in the very next module.

Picasso often made "variations" of other artists' work, and we started out by studying his interpretations of Delacroix and Velázquez in particular. To begin, we studied his words:

> Suppose one were to make a literal copy of *The Maids of Honor*; if it were I, the moment would come when I would say to myself: suppose I moved this figure a little to the right or a little to the left? At that point I would try it without giving a thought to Velázquez. Almost certainly I would be tempted to modify the light or to arrange it differently in view of the changed position of the figure. Gradually, I would create a painting of *The Maids of Honor* sure to

horrify the specialist in the copying of old masters. It would not be *The Maids of Honor* he saw when he looked at Velázquez' picture; it would be *my* Maids of Honor. (Sabartes 1959, p. 6)

We pondered the meaning of these remarks. Someone copied them, and we hung them on the bulletin board to remind us of what Picasso had in mind when he began his reconstructions. He painted fifty-eight studies of *The Maids of Honor,* and we looked at them all. Most are very geometric, composed of lines and angles using a palette of primary colors. First we studied Picasso's faces and painted our own portraits using geometric shapes. Then we experimented with full figures and posed for one another as we tried to capture the essence of a movement with a few strokes. We made our own variations of *The Maids of Honor.* Some students tried to imitate the entire work; others focused on just one figure.

In the library we found a copy of *Children's Homage to Picasso* (Batterberry & Ruskin 1970), which contains fifty-two drawings by Picasso and forty-eight by the children of Vallauris, a town in France near Picasso's home. The drawings are about bullfighting and we found both the drawings and the text of the book to be inspirational. We understood that Picasso dissected the work of other painters in order to learn—to comprehend how and why they had made the decisions that were incorporated into their pictures. In the same spirit we explored Picasso's drawings of matadors and bullfights and sketched our own versions, as the children of Vallauris had done before us.

As a result of studying the variations of *The Maids of Honor,* some of the students asked about Velázquez. We decided that in the next module children could choose to read Elizabeth Borton de Trevino's *I, Juan de Pareja* (1965). Although the book was written more than thirty years ago, it speaks to current issues of race and equity and possibility. Juan de Pareja was the slave willed to Velázquez who learned to paint by studying his master. The portrait of Juan de Pareja that Velázquez painted hangs in the Metropolitan Museum of Art. Although we were not able to go on a class trip to see it, many in the group made special trips with their families to view it on weekends.

The Lincoln Center Institute

We often offered groups called "Lincoln Center," the name of New York City's Center for the Performing Arts. Our school district had become part of the Lincoln Center Institute in the early eighties. Maxine Greene was one of the architects of this program, which was established to help teachers add an aesthetic dimension to their teaching. The Institute brings several hundred teachers to Lincoln Center for three weeks in July to work with performing artists in dance, drama, music, and the visual arts. They participate in morning workshops and view afternoon performances. Teachers, with the help of the artists, explore works of art, put them in historical and cultural contexts, participate in activities designed to identify the aesthetic concepts that characterize the works, and design experiences for children that will enable them to actively explore the same works of art. During the school year, the teaching artists come into the classroom to help prepare students for the performances that are brought to the school. As a result of this program, our students became immersed in the arts.

We particularly enjoyed working with the teaching artists when they came into our school to help us design classes to prepare for an artistic production. We learned a lot from our planning sessions and from working cooperatively with the children to explore the aesthetic elements in the work of art.

When Barbara Ellmann, one of the visual artists from the Lincoln Center Institute, worked with us, she helped us prepare for a trip to the Metropolitan Museum of Art. We specifically planned to visit the Michael C. Rockefeller Wing, which houses art from the Pacific Islands, North and South America, and Africa. In three sessions with the students, Ellmann focused on the characteristics of line, shape, color, and space. We learned that lines have direction, length, and weight. We experimented with charcoal and paper, making drawings composed of lines that were straight and curved, fast and slow, dense and sparse.

Next we worked with geometric and organic shapes as we learned about scale and symmetry. We grouped shapes; overlapped, repeated, and reversed them; and discovered what was meant by negative space.

Then Ellmann introduced color—its value, its intensity, and the concepts of opaque and transparent. We made monochromatic drawings with warm and cool colors. We learned how to combine all of these elements to create texture, rhythm, focus, balance, and contrast. Materials for constructing pictures or sculptures were always available so that students could use them throughout the day when they had the time. Our classroom began to be filled with black-and-white studies of line; twig figures; designs textured with circles, triangles, and squares; white cardboard constructions that small groups produced together; and fascinating experiments in color made with tempera paint and colored chalk.

When it was time for the trip to the museum, we had a vocabulary with which to discuss what we would see and a real understanding of the work of an artist. Students carried notebooks to record shapes, patterns, animals, and their favorite works of art. The informed awareness of what they were viewing enabled the students to more fully comprehend and interact with the works in the exhibition.

In many ways the experience was paradigmatic. Barbara Ellmann modeled the purposefulness, the attention to detail, and the respect for craft that all artists share. The students were inspired to work at new levels of intensity with increased understanding of what it means to be immersed in artistic endeavor.

On another project Miranda Hentoff, a composer and a pianist, introduced us to the work of Zolton Kodaly, a Hungarian composer who lived from 1882 to 1967. We learned the hand signals he developed for the major scale, and we became quite adept at reproducing them as we sang while Miranda conducted. We then read simple two-part melodies based on the scale and graduated to three- and four-part harmonies. In addition to the concept of pitch, we focused on tempo and dynamics.

We were preparing to hear a performance of Haydn's *London Trio #1*, but we had elected to concentrate not so much on the specific performance but rather on a more general understanding of musical composition. What was significant about the unit was the composing work done by the students prior to the performance. We broke them up into groups of five and six and asked them to create, to notate, and then to perform original compositions. This collaborative effort produced several interesting compositions for voice that used the polyphonic and dynamic understandings gained from reading simple scaled melodies with Miranda.

We also worked on making string, wind, and percussive instruments and composing pieces for them. Oatmeal containers became drums, jars filled with beans became maracas, and cigar boxes with rubber bands strung across a hole cut in the middle became guitars. When we were preparing for a performance by the Empire Brass Quintet, we wanted our students to understand how brass instruments work and that a musician must manipulate the mouth and breath to produce a tone. We found that combining a rubber or plastic tube used as the body of an instrument with a kitchen funnel for a bell and an Elmer's glue top as a mouthpiece produced an interesting French horn sound. The fugal pieces that we composed for these instruments helped the children to focus on listening, blending, and keeping time while giving them the experience of ensemble playing. We wanted them to feel that they were a part of a process and a product that could not have been created individually.

What was significant about these units was that we began with a shared experience. We moved from the concrete to the abstract, and as students sang, clapped, and listened they developed new sensitivities and understandings. This aesthetic awareness deepened their appreciation of the concerts they heard as well as opened new windows to classical music in general.

Although New York City is an exciting laboratory for the participants in the Lincoln Center Institute, teachers do not have to travel to New York to experience the mystery and the wonder of the arts. In any school there are parents and community members willing, indeed anxious, to share their expertise. Elementary school teachers can also call upon the resources of the high school by attending their dramatic performances and artistic exhibitions. Engagement with the arts can enrich any school curriculum when teachers are open to the possibilities and have high expectations for their students. Enhanced critical awareness is possible whenever teachers and students together explore the aesthetic dimensions of subject matter. As they listen and look, they will develop the capacity to pay attention to their world in new ways. As Maxine Greene says:

> To engage with works of art is to go in search of fresh connections, unsuspected meanings, to engage in acts of continuing discovery. The more informed these are, the more sensitive we are likely to be to the complexity of the world and the suggestiveness of it, to color and texture and qualities of sound and the relations of shapes in space. Also the more conscious we are likely to be of untapped possibilities. (Greene 1980, p. 8, 9)

Part 3

Essential Elements

Chapter 6

Cooperation and Shared Responsibility

Collaboration

I must admit to a state bordering on hysteria when we first started The Interage Program and I realized I would have to work with two other teachers. Working alone, I had enjoyed a great deal of success as a teacher in the district for more than twenty years. I knew that parents were eager to have me be their children's teacher and that I was equally well respected by my colleagues.

Now I was no longer "in charge." I could not claim complete autonomy. I was about to have to share my classroom, all my belongings, and my ideas and thoughts with my team. I knew there would be a loss of privacy. I wondered if there would be personality clashes. There were bound to be differences in values too.

As it turned out, I had nothing to fear. From the first day the added strength we gained from the shared leadership more than compensated for the losses. But it wasn't always easy. We had to work hard at understanding one another's point of view. We also had to achieve consensus and give up the kind of total control to which we had been accustomed. If we hadn't shared common philosophies and purposes, it would have been impossible. If an issue needed to be worked out, we simply made time to discuss it together. These conversations clarified our sense of purpose and pointed toward heightened awareness of what we must do to achieve our goals.

Just learning to say *we* all the time instead of *I* took time and effort. The *we* sent a message to our students, parents, and administrators that we were a strong, united team speaking as one. Of course, we also agreed ahead of time on what our agenda was and who would carry which message. The *we* also reminded us that we were modeling the importance of collaboration for our students in the the kind of cooperative, conjoint community we were constructing in our classroom.

On two separate occasions, we were asked to add teachers to our team who were experiencing difficulties in their own classrooms. Both stayed with us for two years, retooling and rekindling as well as absorbing the interage approach to teaching. They both used to say that they could never tell when one of us would stop talking and another would start. We always took that as a compliment. We were proud of the fact that our collaboration had enabled us to articulate a clear, consistent philosophy.

There were many obvious advantages to team teaching. We benefitted from companionship, ending the isolation so many teachers endure. We supported one another when we wanted to try out new ideas and explore new ways of teaching, and our brainstorming sessions became times of intense creative interaction. Since we always were being observed informally by one another, we became our own best supervisors. Together we shared ideas about what worked and what failed in our groups. Pooling our resources, both personal and professional, created a more diverse educational environment for us all. Pooling our share of the budget enabled us to collect much richer and more diverse curriculum materials. Furthermore, the flexibility in organizing our time was of great value. We were able to leave the room during emergencies because coverage was always immediately available. We could also have an unscheduled conference with a parent or a colleague if necessary.

The value to our students was of even greater significance. We modeled for them the benefits of cooperation and shared responsibility. We wanted them to see us disagree, and we often demonstrated the way we resolved our own differences by sharing them in public during LGM. We let our students see us arrive at difficult decisions so that they might learn the process of discussion and compromise.

Because we provided three different models for the students, they could profit from three different teaching styles. They had three perspectives to study, three adults from whom to seek counsel or consolation, and sometimes three different views on an issue to contemplate.

Perhaps the greatest benefit of all was the combined perspective we had on the students. When three teachers share their views on the development of a single student, the picture that emerges is richer, more accurate. When one of us might mention an individual student's behavior at the end of the day, we could have that point of view contradicted or reinforced by another team member's account. We simply saw three times as much as any one teacher would be capable of seeing.

This enhanced awareness of our students' development was of special significance when we conferred with parents. While it may have seemed daunting to some, most parents enjoyed the shared perspectives provided when we were all able to attend a conference. The students were also major participants in these conferences. Because of the multi-dimensional portraits that emerged from the combined input of viewpoints, we were able to construct optimal programs and goals.

Together our team created this list of disadvantages and advantages of team-teaching:

Disadvantages

- Lessens maternal/paternal relationship
- Decreases autonomy
- Removes privacy
- Makes decision making more complex
- Requires additional time and organization (sometimes)
- Risks personality differences
- Shares space and materials

Advantages

• Shares responsibility
• Forces intensive look at rationale, theory, goals
• Necessitates a creative use of the environment
• Makes classroom management easier
• Shares problem solving and disciplining
• Strengthens parent conferences
• Makes decision making more democratic, less arbitrary
• Provides supervision by colleagues
• Promotes growth within value differences
• Stimulates development of creative curriculum
• Provides opportunities to teach unfamiliar curriculum with help
• Permits risk taking and exploration
• Makes brainstorming more creative
• Permits flexible groupings, scheduling, planning
• Provides coverage in emergencies
• Pools resources/creates diversity
• Provides companionship/ends isolation
• Models cooperation, collective responsibility
• Affords different perspectives on students
• Aids diagnosis because of multiple views
• Provides more opportunities for individualization
• Deepens student relationships
• Provides a variety of models for students
• Allows students to profit from a variety of teaching styles
• Makes remedial and enrichment programs easier to structure
• Is more fun!

Despite the advantages listed here, team-teaching is not for everyone. We were disappointed when Esther Baranof, the fifth-grade teacher who started with us, decided not to continue after the first year. She found it difficult to adjust to the loss of what we've called a maternal or paternal relationship with her students. They were "our" students—as such, the connection was shared. She remained a strong advocate of the program, however, and incorporated many of its aspects into her own classroom teaching.

It's not easy to team teach. The chemistry has to be right and, even more importantly, the commitments must be equal. Resentments can fester if the work load is not evenly distributed. Perhaps the best combination is like a good marriage. The team members complement one another, and the varied strengths contribute to the stability and integrity of the partnership. Teachers wanting to try team-teaching should begin slowly, perhaps sharing classes for part of one or two days each week. It's a good way to discover if the match will be a successful one.

What is most important, however, is the ability to communicate openly and honestly about problems. Honesty generates respect. Our response to problems was always one of purposeful action to be taken to alleviate tension. Aileen Wissner was especially good at this. She was a sympathetic listener to adults as well as children and was able to ask, "What do you think ought to be done?" at crisis time instead of proffering her own solution. If only more teachers would learn to question as well as they proclaim! A sense of humor helps, too. Barbara Sobolewski kept us laughing even when days were stormy. Her vitality and enthusiasm were contagious!

Community

Our collaboration was an essential ingredient for the success of The Interage Program and the starting point for the creation of a cooperative, mini-community. When we first began planning, we knew we needed to have a sound philosophical base for our endeavors. So we read everything on multiage grouping we could find. In particular, we reread the writings of John Dewey from when he was at the Laboratory School at the University of Chicago. He stressed the notion that school and society are bound together and that there is a relationship between freedom for the individual and the welfare of society. He describes democracy as "primarily a mode of associated living, of conjoint communicated experience" (Dewey 1916, p. 101). The school was the place where capacities could be liberated and shared concerns voiced in an atmosphere of mutual benefit and regard.

As a "little community," the school would saturate children with "the spirit of service" and provide "the instruments of effective self-direction" (Dewey 1899).

This notion of a community built on service and self-direction became a guiding concept for us. We wanted to establish a close-knit, supportive community where students as well as teachers could become risk-takers and experimenters. We also wanted to include parents as fully as possible as members of the community. In chapter 7, you will read about the many ways they participated in the program.

Some of our colleagues questioned us about this and honestly thought they couldn't realistically involve their students to such a degree. We found, however, that when we shared our decision-making processes with students and parents, we learned a great deal. Their collaboration and commensurate support empowered us to take risks more easily and to explore curriculum innovation and experiment with flexible groupings. In our discussions we were endlessly reviewing our goals and aspirations, and the multiple perspectives on problemsolving always opened new vistas.

Our students were not isolated from the rest of the school. They ate in the cafeteria and played on the playground after lunch. As a matter of fact, it was in these areas that what trouble we did have most often erupted. We tried to use such incidents to stress the possibilities for leadership. We would ask children from other classes to join us in a discussion so that differences could be resolved.

In the beginning we often resented the extra effort it took to negotiate better relationships with other classes that did not have the same background in shaping rules of behavior. But our class had a reputation for fairness and patience, and it required less and less time on our part as the children learned to handle those situations on their own as they occurred. A school psychologist eventually taught a group on conflict resolution for us and used those children whom she trained as helpers on the playground.

A teacher has to be careful here. In stressing service and self-direction in a classroom, there is the danger of developing an elitist attitude among students. We wanted our students to think that they were not only capable and competent but also fortunate to have the opportunities for personal growth and development that we were providing. At the same time we did not want them to think that students in other classes were less fortunate. Guarding against this superior attitude took time and patience. What we tried to develop was the sense that our students were members of several overlapping communities. We used Venn diagrams to illustrate the ways in which they were connected to the classroom, to the school, and to society. If children begin at an early age to understand these interrelationships, they should be better able to function in all three.

Large Group Meetings

As we've mentioned briefly, the forum for the exchange of ideas, information, and perspectives was called the Large Group Meeting. It was here that we gathered together to give voice to all the members of the community. We discussed the ways in which the ideas of service and self-direction were in evidence, we participated in democratic government, we shared our collaborative endeavors and celebrated their successful achievement, and we handed down our accumulating history. The LGM, as we called it, became the heart of our program. It was vital to the agreement of principles we could live by and essential for the sharing of ideas and the exploration of our diversity.

The rules of the classroom had been developed by the students at a Large Group Meeting, and the voice they had in their establishment did more to discourage disruptive behavior than any teacher's voice could have. When infractions occurred we would often hear students reminding each other of the rules they had devised. And when teachers had to intervene, it was helpful to point to the list and remind angry children that they had voted on each of the points on it. At the same time we were reminding our students that they were free to disagree, that there was not always one right answer, and that shared decision making was part of The Interage Program.

The LGM wasn't simply a time for rule formation and disciplinary action. We also needed to determine how well our community was functioning. We discussed the decisions our students were being asked to make and the rights and responsibilities that choice making and risk taking entailed. We often asked if anyone had seen a classmate helping another student in some way or if anyone had been helped by a classmate. We were also careful to stress the importance of service to the whole school community as well as to our own.

The LGM also provided the opportunity to discuss themes and concepts that were emerging from our studies or from current events. We often read picture books to stimulate the discussion because they are wonderfully crafted short stories that offer both inspiration and example to budding authors. We used such old favorites as *Leo the Late Bloomer* (Kraus 1971) and *Crow Boy* (Yashima 1955) to discuss developmental differences. *The Hundred Dresses* (Estes 1944) and *Molly's Pilgrim* (Cohen 1983) were helpful in exploring prejudice. These books gave us the opportunity to achieve new insights into the goals we had established for the community.

Our students were encouraged to share their own stories too. Children are always perfect audiences when other children perform. As they would listen to recently completed stories and poems, you could almost feel the degree of concentration and the recognition and appreciation for the authors' endeavors. Students always gave credit to classmates who had provided inspiration.

The LGM was the time for sharing completed projects, for summarizing work that had been done in the study groups, and for performing plays and skits. We held "news broadcasts" on Fridays. These were patterned after network newscasts and provided weather, sports, commercials, and information about international, national, and local events. Because of these broadcasts, I always knew more about sports than anyone in my family. And the commercials students devised for imaginary products were usually hysterical.

One of our "weathermen," Tommy, memorized the map of the United States. Each week he quickly sketched an outline of the country on the blackboard (accompanied by ohs and ahs because of his accuracy) and then pointed to the general location of various states as he recited the forecast. His knowledge of geography was so impressive that he motivated everyone else to try to memorize the location of each state.

We could also use our small stage during LGM to present more formal programs. Often we would invite other classes. On Dr. Martin Luther King's birthday, for example, we invited all the primary classes to a short play about his life. Then we discussed nonviolence and sang "We Shall Overcome." The total absorption of the audience again reminded us that children are often the best teachers of other children and that a sense of community can best be felt through conjoint communication and experiences.

Chapter 7

Teaching Others to Teach

When we started The Interage Program we believed that it was essential to create strong relationships between and among the participants: students, parents, and teachers. We recognized that the education of a child was a continuum begun in the home and continued in the school. Eliminating unnecessary divisions between home and school was a strong priority. Students lived in both worlds and needed to feel their connectedness; parents needed to feel that they had a voice in what was occurring in the school; teachers needed to feel that their work in the school was understood and supported at home. Not only did we want our students to be the architects of their own educational experiences, we also wanted the parents to feel involved and committed. We knew we needed their support as well as their guidance.

Parent Meetings

Too often we had witnessed the stress that occurs when there are basic disagreements between schools and parents. Teachers often do not realize the conflicts that can result in the home when what the school is trying to accomplish is at odds with the values of the parents. And parents who engage in angry conversations with school personnel cannot fathom the anxiety they create in teachers. The unfortunate consequence is that the child, caught in the middle of two loyalties, suffers the most.

In the first years of the program, parents were given the option to place their children with us. That ensured a commitment to the kind of education we provided. In later years, when demand for places exceeded capacity, we were disappointed that the administration was no longer able to offer choice of placement to parents. Instead, they decided to assign children to classes on the basis of recommendations made by committees of teachers. That made a difference in some parents' attitudes. Those who otherwise might not have requested the program lacked enthusiasm, and others who wanted their children in the program but did not gain access felt resentment. Although the administration had the final say, we remained committed to the idea of allowing parents to have a voice in the placement of their children, just as we remained committed to allowing students in The Interage Program to choose their differing paths to learning.

First Meeting

We always scheduled a parent meeting for the first week of school so that parents of all new students would have a clear understanding of what The Interage Program was all about and what the first module would bring. We also felt it was important to ask for their support and to urge them to communicate directly and immediately if any problem arose. We cautioned them that progress comes in spurts and that after an initial burst of energy and excitement, there might be a period of lessened activity on the part of their children. We conducted the meeting in much the same way that we introduced the new module to the students, going over the content of each study group and describing the commitments that each child would make as a result of choosing a specific group. We also explained that in our view, curriculum should provide experiences that would enable children to be active participants in their learning. It should draw on their interests while developing new ones and, at the same time, point out connections between subject matter areas. We demonstrated the range and complexity of the possibilities for each study, and demonstrated the ways in which we might consider developing a thematic unit.

Interestingly enough, most of the parents of our returning students also came to this meeting. They told us that they loved to hear the excitement in our voices as we talked about what the first module would be like and that they didn't want to wait until the Open House in October to see us. We were grateful for their loyalty and support. The new students' parents often asked how we were able to continue to challenge the older pupils. As soon as this issue came up, the older students' parents would explain that the third year in the program was the most satisfying of all because of the students' increased independence, their commitment to learning, and their motivation to pursue in-depth studies. The returning parents were enormously influential. For the new parents, this was the first step in becoming a member of the interage community.

Open House

At the Open House in October, we went over the curriculum. We explained what would be covered in all the subject matter areas and did some demonstration teaching in math or in science. The room was always decorated for the occasion with examples of finished projects and work-in-progress. We always left lots of time for parent questions and, as a result, often explored broader educational issues. Lively discussions often ensued. There was sometimes a political edge to these discussions; there was always a strong demonstration of community support for excellence in education.

Spring Walk-Through

During April the whole school had a "Spring Walk-Through." This was similar to an open house, but this time the children were invited. Whole families toured the school building and stopped to chat with the classroom teachers. Children were able to introduce parents to special area teachers they might not ordinarily meet. The school became a magical place. Walls were lined with studies and projects representing many months of work, and halls were filled with the laughter of children and the gasps of appreciation of the parents. One sensed strong circles of friendship and community on these evenings. We loved them.

Parent Conferences

In addition to these large school meetings, teachers regularly scheduled two conferences a year with individual parents. We scheduled these throughout the year, both in the morning and after school, depending on what was most convenient for parents. It is important to note, however, that we had informal conferences with the parents all year long. Because they felt welcome in our classroom at all times, we often met for a few moments to exchange a word or two when there were questions about a child's development. In the first school in which we were housed, we even had a telephone in the classroom. Parents could call us directly or we could phone them in the mornings or after school. That was a great convenience. It was eventually removed, but it made us aware of the advantages of direct telephone contact with parents.

Almost without exception, conferences were never held without the student being present. Again, the connection between school and home was made, students felt that nothing was being decided behind their backs, the sense of commitment on the part of the students was increased, and the goals agreed upon at the conference were identified by the students in conjunction with the parents and the teachers.

Parents as Teachers

What really helped us bridge the gap between school and home was the presence of parents as teachers in our classroom. We asked for volunteers at the beginning of each year and offered them consultations if necessary about the organization of subject matter and classroom management. We wanted students to understand that the school was not separated from real life and that the skills, attitudes, and understandings they were gaining were connected to the world outside the school. Parents not only provided alternative role models for our students, they also increased the ratio of adults in the classroom and the number of choices available for children.

Over the years, many of the parents who volunteered to work with us decided to go back to school to study education. Just as we have shared in the success of our students, so have we watched these parents become caring and committed teachers.

We began by inviting authors among the parent group to come to talk with us about writing and to share their ongoing work. We were fortunate to always have two or three parents who were writers. Often they were children's authors, which made it even more exciting. One parent, who writes interesting, informative books about science brought galley proofs of his latest book and explained to us the process of editing. Another was an editor of the local newspaper, and she helped us begin a class newspaper.

A sculptor gave us lessons in ceramics and invited us to her studio to see her work-in-progress. An artist helped us make huge paper sculptures from scraps of colorful cardboard salvaged from a local picture-framing store. Many parents helped with scenery and costumes for our Gilbert and Sullivan performances. One played the piano for us at every rehearsal and performance for six years!

A firefighter who had two daughters in the program came several times to talk about his work and about safety precautions in the home. One mother who was a dental assistant came every year to instruct children on good dental care. She brought packages of dental floss and toothbrushes for all the students. Another who was a secondary school math teacher on leave taught advanced classes in algebra and geometry for us for a whole year.

We almost always had parents come in to conduct cooking groups. We often tied these groups to cultural and historic studies. One year we baked different breads from around the world every week and filled the nearby corridors with its delicious scents.

By including parents in the teaching process, we found we were able to offer a great variety of foreign languages. We had study groups on Spanish, French, Italian, Latin, Hebrew, and Farsi. The children learned basic vocabulary, songs and poetry, and then studied the cultures where each language was spoken. They also did a lot of cooking and tasting of regional dishes. I often taught Italian, and nothing motivated the children more than the Italian words such as *lasagna*, *spaghetti*, and *pizza* that our language has adopted—of course, we had to learn how to prepare each one!

Some parents came to class only once during the year to share a hobby or to show slides. Others could set aside an hour each week to teach in a six-week module. A lawyer taught courtroom procedure to her group and then conducted a mock trial to try Goldilocks for breaking and entering. A physician taught a unit on germs and set up Petri dishes filled with nothing more than the breath of each student. As the dishes grew colorful and intriguing bacterial and fungal forms, the children examined them under a microscope, drew what they observed, and magnified them for display.

A pathologist brought slides and vivisections of diseased lungs to his group on physiology. A healthy lung should be a soft beige color, but the lung of a city dweller was dark brown. When the children saw the jet black lung of a smoker the impact was staggering.

Not all parents could participate in such a way, and we explained that carefully to students and parents several times a year. We wanted to be sure that no one had resentments when parents were unable to take time off from work. One father who worked in the financial district and wanted very much to be a part of the program managed to slip away on his lunch hour to meet us at the Whitney Museum of Art in New York City. He accompanied us on our tour and felt satisfied to fulfill a familial obligation while snatching an aesthetic moment from a busy day.

We spent a lot of time in The Interage Program celebrating our differences as well as our similarities. We were always happy to have children from special classes join us for portions of their day, because we wanted our students to respect and admire them. No one helped our students to understand the nature of a disability more than the mother who was raised by parents who were both deaf and mute. Each year she taught a group on sign language, peppering her discussions with stories of her own unusual childhood. When the students had mastered the basics of signing, she would invite her parents to visit and to "converse" with the class. Because she had three sons, all of whom were in our program at one time or other, we had the benefit of her teaching for nine years! We watched her parents delight in new technologies and mourned with her the death of her father. We were, indeed, all one extended family.

One mother co-taught a study group on Asian culture with her son. In a written summary she wrote:

> My son had excellent ideas on what subjects would stimulate, interest and challenge the class . . . "Asian Adventures" involved history, geography, culture, and art of the Asian countries. Mark and I selected several maps for the group to complete to learn country placement and capitals. We asked each student to read a folk tale from an Asian country and do a full page report. Mark took the students to the school library, where selections were already pulled, and since he was familiar with many stories, he helped them choose the books.
>
> We also did several art projects such as origami, Chinese rubbings, cooking, writing Chinese characters, etc. The students were able to benefit when Mark and I assisted them, and Mark had some "one-to-one" sessions to help with origami.
>
> To summarize, I was able to learn a great deal from the team teaching because I saw Mark's growth in mastering subject matter and learning processes expand. He developed confidence and the ability to speak in front of a group. The students prospered by learning new information and skills from a peer and to respect a fellow student. I gained the insight of seeing how important it is to know your student audience, their needs and capabilities. By treating the students as individuals and demanding quality work, I saw they were capable of learning much more than I would have expected from a third, fourth, or fifth grader.

The entire interaction was very positive and the information shared was valuable to all of us.

Students as Teachers

Mark was not the only student who taught in The Interage Program, although he was one of the few who teamed with his mother to do so. We regularly encouraged our students to take on the responsibility for researching and planning an instructional unit on a topic of their choice. Most students elected to do this at least once in the three years they were with us.

We had two main reasons for encouraging them to do so. First, teaching provides opportunities for learning. As teachers, we learned a great deal by teaching a study group. If, for example, I was going to offer a unit on the Etruscans, I would spend at least two weeks gathering materials and rereading books and articles that I had collected. I did this automatically even though I have spent a lot of time in Italy poking around the Tuscan countryside and have gathered a good deal of material on this pre-Roman civilization. I wanted to be prepared for any direction our studies would take us and to be able to direct students to information that they might need. As we encouraged our students to teach, we wanted them to experience the same excitement we felt when we prepared to teach, and we wanted them to realize how much one could learn in undertaking these investigations.

The other lesson to be learned was more subtle, and we discovered it after listening to students talk about their teaching experiences. Not until they had the responsibility for organizing and instructing their fellow classmates did they truly understand and appreciate the process of teaching and, therefore, the process of learning. They seemed to become better listeners because they understood what it was like when someone didn't pay attention. They were more conscientious about their own assignments after they'd experienced the frustration of receiving unfinished homework. Most important, we felt they gained a broader understanding of the differences among their classmates and a heightened awareness of their individual needs.

The "kids' groups," as we called them, were as varied as their parents' groups. Some were related to particular interests or hobbies, such as stamp collecting or ballet dancing. Others were patterned after teacher-led groups in which they had been participants. Others were related to in-depth studies the students were pursuing. Here is the list of groups offered by students for one half-year:

Famous Presidents
Electrons
Puzzles
Minerals
Edgar A. Poe
Kids' Critics
Maps
Food and Countries
Consumerism
Castles
Dance

Some youngsters, especially those new to the program, were anxious to teach but didn't know where to begin. For these and for some of the older students too, we organized a study group called "How To Have a Group." This was basically an independent research seminar. Students thought about their interests and their questions, decided upon a topic, made a list of possible resources, gathered books and articles from both the school and the public libraries, shared their findings with the group, and made an outline of the topics they would cover in each session. In effect, they became experts.

While they were pursuing these investigations, the group as a whole would discuss methodology and management. Depending on whether the group they might teach would meet once or twice a week, they had to plan either six or twelve lessons. Decisions about team-teaching also had to be made. Some preferred to work alone; others welcomed the shared responsibility. We shared our own organizational tips with these students, such as keeping all the materials for a particular mini-course in colorful plastic dishpans and keeping records of attendance and completed homework on special class lists. We were always amused to see these students carrying their dishpans to a meeting. And when we observed their classes we would marvel at their efficiency in collecting assignments.

More important, we shared the ways in which we were able to individualize our teaching. We taught them to respect the different levels that they would find in their classes and helped them to understand the importance of having each student set realistic goals for the six weeks. They knew that their job was to help their students choose projects and reach their objectives. It was their responsibility to provide the kind of support that would enable their group to achieve success.

There was always a lot of discussion about activities. The students were anxious to present interesting and exciting experiences to their classmates so that someone would sign up for their group. Usually the biggest draw was cooking. It was often difficult for many of these students-who-would-be-teachers to find the proper balance between entertainment and learning. I suppose, however, that the same is true for many of us in the profession.

Here, for example, is a plan submitted by two girls for approval:

Ice Cream Around the World

Week 1
Talk about different kinds of ice cream. We will ask the group what their favorite kind of ice cream is.
    Homework=None

Week 2
We will talk about the man or boy who invented ice cream
    Homework=None

Week 3
Tell them that they have a report due in 3 weeks; ask them what ice cream they are doing. Discuss how ice cream was made and discuss the products.
    Homework=Start report

Week 4
Let them work on the report in class.
    Homework=Do some if you like

Week 5
Play ice cream bingo using ice cream facts that they can learn about.
    Homework=try to finish the rest of the report.

Week 6
If anyone's report is finished share it with the group.
    Homework=None

Week 7
Play bingo game, ice cream trivia, and hand out prizes (everyone gets one)

Week 8
Talk about the different ways ice cream is eaten & made
    Homework=None

Week 9
Talk about the favorite ice cream and what flavor we'll make at the end.
    Homework=None

Week 10
Make a big ice cream cone and play pin the cherry on the ice cream top.

Week 11
Tell them to wear raggy clothes because next time we're making ice cream. Read reports out loud.

Week 12
Have our parents come in and make ice cream.

While we applauded the attempt to make the learning "relevant," we rejected this plan and asked the girls to join the "How to Have a Group" course. Two modules later, when they had completed it, they received permission for a revised ice cream project. It ran for six sessions, included research activities and oral and written reports about ice cream in various cultures, and concluded with a party in which the group, not the parents, made and served the whole class homemade ice cream. It was delicious!

We also emphasized questioning techniques whenever we were teaching others to teach. We discussed the difference between the questions intended to help children recall the facts and events in a story or the steps in an experiment and the in-depth questions that required analysis and evaluation and might have more than one right answer. More often than not, we asked students to write and answer their own questions as a follow-up to a lesson.

Whenever the children taught a mini-course based on a book that would be shared, we hoped that their questions would be interesting and provocative. Here, for example, are the questions submitted by two girls who requested permission to teach a book by Patricia MacLachlan (1985). The written work was planned so that each student teacher could check on the progress and the level of understanding of each member of her group:

> Over the module we would like to teach a group. The book that we will be reading is called *Sarah, Plain and Tall*. We will read the book in six weeks and this is what we have planed. The first week we will pass out books and begin to read. The second week we will read some more and discuss the book. The third week in the group we will all draw pictures of our favorite character so far in the book and tell why we like them. The fourth week we will read and discuss the book. The fifth week we will finish the book. Homework: Write a short summary of the book. Sixth week: We will share our summaries.
>
> 1. How did Sarah feel about leaving the sea? And why?
> 2. How did the children feel when Sarah came?

3. Did the children think that they would like Sarah right away, when she came? How could you tell?

4. Did Sarah like the family right away, when she came? How could you tell?

5. Describe Sarah?

6. Describe Anna?

7. How do you think Caleb felt not really knowing his mother?

8. How do you think Anna felt when she answered all of Caleb's question about their mother?

9. Sarah might become Anna and Caleb's mother. What qualities are important to Caleb and Anna in a mother?

10. Do you think that Papa knows how important a mother is to Anna and Caleb? (give reasons)

11. Is Papa happy with Sarah? How could you tell?

12. Anna and Caleb both wrote letters to Sarah. Do you think Sarah could tell from the letters how much Anna and Caleb wanted a mother?

13. Do you think Papa, Sarah, Anna and Caleb make a good family? Tell why?

Both girls recently had chosen to take a mini-course based on this book and had liked it so much they decided to invite a new group of students to join them in reading it. This was not unusual. We realized that we were often modeling for future teachers each time we taught. We always took it as a compliment if students in our classes asked to re-teach a course in a subsequent module. And we also knew that by doing so, they would truly make the material their own.

The process of students teaching other students was very satisfying to us as teachers. In some modules we would schedule all the student-taught groups during one period. For us to stand in the middle of the room and see as many as six groups huddled around the student leaders, intently discussing a topic without a teacher, was most gratifying. I still can feel the electricity in that air and can remember vividly the sense of personal satisfaction that comes when you are able to step aside and let students learn independently.

Part 4

Assessment and Evaluation

Chapter 8

Student Assessment

Teacher–Student Conferences

To make The Interage Program a success, we knew we had to know our students well and be able to document their growth accurately and effectively. The school system administered the California Test of Basic Skills each spring. In addition, the State of New York required the Degree of Reading Power for third graders, the Elementary Science Program Evaluation Test (ESPET) for fourth graders, and a writing test for fifth graders. While each of these tests evaluates certain ability levels, we wanted assessment of our students to be comprehensive, continuous, and self-initiated whenever appropriate.

One of the most effective ways to achieve this was to have a regularly scheduled weekly conference with each child built right into the schedule. In these individual conferences, we were able to differentiate instruction, initiate diagnostic or corrective projects, and plan for future activities. We divided the class in three heterogenous parts: the reds, blues, and greens. Each teacher was assigned to a group and was responsible for seeing each of those students at least once a week. If necessary, she could schedule an additional meeting. Halfway through the year, we switched conference teachers by redistributing the color code. That meant that each teacher saw two-thirds of the class each year. Over the course of a year and a half, she would conference with all the students in the program.

We had originally thought that we might switch groups three times a year so that each of us could confer with all the children

	Monday	Tuesday	Wednesday	Thursday	Friday
9:30	Gym: Blues & Reds Music: Greens Preparation Period	Gym: Reds & Greens Music: Blues Preparation Period	Art: Reds Shop: Blues Science: Greens Preparation Period	Gym: Blues & Greens Music: Reds Preparation Period	LGM Preparation Period
10:15	––––	Math	Math	Math	Math
11:05	––––	Mammals	Newsprint	Mammals	Newsprint
12:00	Lunch	Lunch	Lunch	Lunch	Lunch
1:10	–––– READING AND CONFERENCES	–––– READING AND CONFERENCES	–––– READING AND CONFERENCES	–––– READING AND CONFERENCES	–––– READING AND CONFERENCES
2:15	The Bill of Rights	The Romans	Science Fiction	The Romans	Science Fiction

Figure 8–1 Sample Module Schedule

in one year. But we decided that we needed to have more continuity in the communication taking place at the conferences and we found that half a year was an ideal length of time. It provided the needed intensity but also allowed for a change of pace when the changeover occurred. Just as the change of offerings in each new module provided children with a feeling of renewal, so did the change of conference teacher. And the change was equally beneficial for the teachers.

We built time for these conferences into our regular schedule. Some took place during the quiet reading time, others during a period when we were not scheduled to teach. It was not unusual for us to run overtime in a conference, but if that made us miss seeing a student, we could usually schedule an appointment later in the day. We left time in our own schedules for this (see Figure 8-1). I would post this in the classroom and students could select a conference time by penciling in their name on one of the blank lines.

The conferences generally lasted about fifteen or twenty minutes and took place at the same location each week. Students knew exactly where to find their conference teacher and were expected to be ready at the appointed time. They carried a reminder in their notebooks that asked them to bring their schedules, logs, assignments, books that they were currently reading, and anything they needed help with.

The conference was primarily a time for sharing. We generally began with the journal. We read the week's entries, commented on them, worked on any mechanics or grammar instruction that seemed necessary, and talked about any problems connected with writing a daily entry. The log was also the primary means of assessment in all curricular areas because responses to math lessons or science experiments were always included. We could check for standards, for in-depth understanding, or for misunderstandings. We would often refer back to entries made at the beginning of the year to point out growth or to compare approaches to learning over time.

We had stressed that this log was not meant to be a confidential document, so students were always willing to share the contents. We also encouraged students to share the logs with parents. We thought it was a wonderful form of communication between the school and the home—a kind of continuous progress report.

At the conference we also examined the schedule, asking about the groups the student had chosen for that module. We looked over any assignments, helped with difficulties, and offered assistance when needed. This was often the occasion for reteaching if students had a problem with skills or concepts that had been taught in one of the groups. We could devise a quick, informal diagnostic test to check understanding and provide students with the opportunity for one-to-one tutoring if it was necessary.

We also discussed the independent reading that the students were doing and suggested new books that would interest them. If there was time, we asked students to read aloud favorite passages. We often moved such book discussions to the book room so we could pull recommended titles from the shelves more easily and send students off with two or three books from which to choose.

During the conferences, we also made notes in folders that were filed in the teachers' work space. These were not generally available for student perusal. We did, however, often share what we had recorded at the conferences, and students were encouraged to add anything they thought appropriate to their folder. These folders not only contained a record of each conference, but they also held accumulated schedules, reading autobiographies, in-class test results, anecdotal notes about students' work or behavior, parent communications, students' half-year evaluations of their own progress, copies of report cards, and samples of work.

Throughout the year we tried never to use a deficit model with our students. We ended conferences with a query about new goals for the week so that students would learn to set their own standards and targets. At every opportunity we reminded them that they were the architects of their own learning experiences. It was not easy to do this, but by the end of their third year they became quite articulate in assessing their accomplishments and identifying their goals.

Teacher–Parent–Student Conferences

We scheduled regular conferences with parents twice a year, although we often had many more than two. This was our major way of informing parents of their children's progress, but we also liked to think of it as a time for parents to tell us what they thought we needed to know.

Students were invited to all conferences—we considered their presence an absolute necessity. That idea was difficult for some parents in the beginning. They would ask how it would be possible to discuss anything openly with the child present. We would ask what their experience with conferences had been and if they had, in fact, ever discussed anything that they didn't later report to their child. The answer was almost always that nothing had ever been said that the child could not hear. We also assured parents that if they had anything confidential to report to us, we would certainly be available for a second private conference or a phone call.

Some of the students who were newcomers to The Interage Program also found it difficult to meet with their teachers and parents. They had never had the opportunity to participate in a conference before, and they usually just listened to most of the discussion. By the time the students had been in the program for three years, however, they were really in charge of the parent conferences. They not only were able to articulate their goals and explain their accomplishments, but they also were able to evaluate their programs and point to new directions for themselves.

Occasionally, other teachers would join us, and often all three of the regular teachers would sit in on the conference. That was really fun, and with three adults present who had monitored growth and achievement, we were able to provide parents with the rich picture we had of each student.

Previous to the conference, the class prepared written evaluations of the year to date. We gave them a prompt that asked questions about all aspects of their work in The Interage Program:

How have I helped others this year? Have I helped my class?
Do I get my work done on time?
Am I a good listener at LGM? In groups? In kids' groups?
Do I follow directions?
What do I want to learn about before June?
How much do I read? What kinds of books do I like best?
Do I ask questions when I feel I don't understand something?
Do I like writing in my log? Do I feel my writing has improved?
Do I respect the rights and property of others? Do I feel others respect my rights?
Am I a patient and understanding friend? Do I have friends in the interage? Have I made new friends?
Do I follow directions?
Do I have confidence in myself?
What are the things I like best about school? What do I like least?
What do I want to learn about before June?

These questions varied from year to year and were meant to be only guides for the narratives that the students wrote. The final copies were mailed home to parents, but the draft copies were kept in the individual folders and became additional documents that tracked progress over time for each student.

The district also required that we use a report card once a year. We used a form that allowed children to evaluate their own performance. Like most such reporting procedures, the curricular areas were listed next to three columns. Our columns were labeled *needs improvement, satisfactory,* and *a strength.* We told our class first to check the six or seven things that they thought they needed to improve, and then the six or seven things that they thought they excelled in. The rest of the check marks would probably fit in the middle category. We also included spaces for teacher comments in each area of the curriculum.

For the most part, this was a successful procedure (or, as successful as report cards ever can be). We usually sent them home right before the spring conference. As much as possible, we tried to inhibit the onerous comparisons that youngsters are apt to engage in. We reviewed the cards at the conference, discussing the ways in which the students saw themselves as learners. Often, some students marked all the categories *a strength*. We would call attention to the fact that this marked a healthy sense of self and a high degree of confidence, and then turn to a discussion of new goals and possibilities. Conversely, some students checked everything in the *needs improvement* category. We would call attention to the fact that those students obviously set very high standards for themselves and then discuss what they had already achieved.

In other words, the "grades" students gave themselves were irrelevant if the conference accomplished what it was meant to accomplish. We tried to be informed, knowledgeable, and positive in our classroom, and we wanted the parents to feel informed, knowledgeable, and positive when they left the conference. We asked the students to share their evaluation of the year to date and to talk about their goals for the remainder of the year. We shared test scores if there were any, papers from the groups that each student had attended, and examples of work completed in special areas such as art or music.

Teacher–Teacher Conferences

Evaluation of the students in The Interage Program was continuous. We made informal observations all day long and took the time to share insights with one another whenever possible. Sometimes we simply made comments to one another as we passed on the way to a group meeting. Most often we spent time before and after school sharing insights and experiences and profiting from one another's expertise.

It seemed sometimes as though we could go on forever talking about our students, our program, our plans. We ate lunch together every day because we had so much to share.

This is an important component of team-teaching that contributes to the success of both the teachers and the students. Teachers learn from one another in a way that is not possible when one is isolated in a classroom. We constantly struggled to find better ways to listen, to communicate, to motivate, and to differentiate instruction. Often, solutions were found in these informal exchanges as we batted around ideas. In that sense, we were our own best supervisors. Students also benefitted from the combined perspectives of three professionals. The understanding that we gained from shared portraits of learners and effective ways of working with them were invaluable.

Chapter 9

Evaluation of the Program

Just as the assessment of our students was continual, so was the evaluation of the program as a whole. We stopped to question how things were going at the end of each LGM, each day, each module, and each year. We looked at ourselves, each other, and the consultants. We sought feedback from the parents, other teachers, and former students. All of this was done informally, although we had asked for a formal evaluation from time to time.

When parents began to question the way in which students were admitted to our program, some discussion ensued about the heterogeneity of the group and about the admission of siblings. There was a perception among some parents that the most able students were assigned to The Interage Program, and there was also some negative reaction to the fact that siblings had been given preference for admission.

The policy for admission had changed over the years. Originally almost all of the parental requests were honored. After five years, two teachers launched a second interage program at the school, so for awhile there were enough placements for all who wanted their children to have such an experience.

Unfortunately, as the demand for the program continued to grow, the administration decided to eliminate parental request and instead allow a committee of teachers to choose children with gender and ability equity to fill the requisite number of groups for the following year.

We were not pleased with this arrangement because we felt that our program depended on strong parental support and involvement. In fact, the success of any program depends on parental backing, and any teacher has to win the allegiance of both her students and the parents. But even though the groups were constructed by the regular teachers, the impression persisted among some teachers and parents that the more able students were assigned to The Interage Program.

The preference that had been given to the brothers and sisters of former interage students was also deemed discriminatory and eliminated. We had argued in favor of this practice because we thought it seemed unfair for a sibling to hear about the program every night at the dinner table for three years and then not be able to participate in it when he or she reached the proper age. Again, our arguments were overruled.

This tension is not unusual for a special program housed within a larger school. Although we never were referred to as a "school-within-a-school," we were sufficiently different and independent to warrant that assumption by many teachers and parents, who questioned the equitable distribution of resources such as special monies, equipment, or teaching materials, and the equitable distribution of students. These were among the issues that prompted the Board of Education to initiate a formal evaluation of The Interage Program in 1988. The principal investigator was Dr. Mary Anne Raywid from the Administration and Policy Studies Department of Hofstra University. She called on several consultants, including Dr. Robert Anderson, co-author of *The Nongraded Elementary School* (1963); Deborah Meier, at that time principal of Central Park East School in New York City; Ann Cook, principal of The Urban Academy in New York City; and Dr. JoAnn Shaheen, Director of Elementary Education in Blauvelt, New York. Dr. Raywid's report was presented to the Board at a special meeting in January of 1989.

The Outside Evaluators

All the experts were positive in their evaluations. The report points out that they found that many of the reforms being urged for education today were already in place: a stimulating environment; an interdisciplinary, literature-based curriculum; cooperative learning; active learner participation and lack of "busy work"; intellectual purposefulness; higher level questioning and critical thinking; an emphasis on values. They also noted the organizational characteristics that gave strength to the program: the fact that we were a multiage, multiyear classroom using team-teaching; that we had created a cohesive group; and that we enjoyed the freedom to make decisions and define the program.

Here are some quotes from Deborah Meier, found in the report to the district:

> The three women I met were among the most extraordinarily clear and level-headed professionals I've recently encountered. They loved their work, knew their kids and subjects well, felt comfortable wearing many different academic hats, had high standards for acceptable work and had communicated clear criteria to kids. They had created a program with a quality of consistence and integrity that is the mark of a good classroom.
>
> I interviewed many of the students and was impressed with their explanation of their work and their acceptance of the idea that challenging work was the best kind (they seemed baffled at my query whether choice sometimes led to picking easier work). They insisted that age differences were unimportant, and that learning new things was wonderful. They all showed me lots of written work, carefully reviewed and edited; they enjoyed being provoked into reexamining their ideas in math—without defensiveness or anxiety. They listened when spoken to, were quiet during quiet times, moved about with assurance when that was appropriate. They were unfailingly courteous. Imagine that! (Raywid 1989, p. 80)

Dr. Shaheen commented on the classroom environment:

> There was a sense of ease in the classroom. Everyone seemed to be respected, including children across grade levels and teachers. Each child seemed to feel accountable for his/her learning, and, yet, there was a sense of joy and of ease which pervaded the classroom. It was as if the clock did not dictate compartmentalized learning. There

was a sense of children learning skills, knowledge, and attitudes, of integrated learning, of children *learning* rather than children *being taught* reading and mathematics. This integration may account, in part, for the higher knowledge levels in science and social studies which I observed and heard.(Raywid 1989, p. 83)

She also cited nine characteristics and practices that she found to be "in accordance with the best of our knowledge and research about effective learning":

1. There is obviously a highly preplanned curriculum.

2. There are high teacher expectations for student learning and for the development of positive attitudes toward learning, self, and others.

3. Students seem to be carefully oriented to lessons with help in getting started, in understanding clear objectives, and in having appropriate academic challenges.

4. Instruction is clear, focused, and progress is monitored formally and informally in very close ways.

5. The classroom is used for learning, and routines support this because they are smooth, efficient, and clearly understood by children.

6. Children and teachers seem constantly to be sensitive to the need for instruction.

7. At a time in our nation when citizens and educators are concerned about valueless classrooms, the students in this classroom are living in ways which provide daily lessons in responsibility, freedom, friendliness, acceptance of diversity, fairness, honesty, and cooperation.

8. The interactions between teachers and students were among the most positive I have seen.

9. While there are extrinsic rewards and incentives to promote excellence, I felt that the real incentive was coming from students who understood that they personally gain in important ways when they seek to learn and to accomplish. (Quite an accomplishment for eight-, nine-, and ten-year-olds.) (Raywid 1989, pp. 83, 84)

Ann Cook pointed to many of the benefits of team teaching:

From several pedagogical perspectives, this interage program makes the most of teacher teaming. In addition to eliminating the isolation so often felt by teachers who teach self-contained classrooms, the team is able to discuss and plan for the students from three different points of view. Listening to the staff members integrate what they knew about students, curriculum and current research made it evident that there is a consistent sharing and working through of ideas. The staff discussion followed by this observer further indicated that the staff drew on one another's strengths in ways impossible in a traditional classroom environment.

Perhaps equally important, is the learning opportunity teaming allows for in the classroom. In traditional classrooms students seldom have the opportunity to hear divergent points of view on important topics. Rarely, do classrooms provide for a clash of ideas, or modeling of good argument and healthy disagreement.

Children need to experience real dialogue in order to be able to do it themselves. They need to hear unpopular views represented in reasoned and thoughtful ways. Having three adults to take positions, to argue and marshall evidence is of critical importance for it forces students to consider views other than their own and helps them begin to examine their own opinions within the context of a supportive atmosphere. In The Interage Program's Large Group Meeting, such learning opportunities are not only possible but are part of the ongoing curriculum.

This interage program is pioneering learning possibilities for students. To this observer, it seems a model for school, teachers and parents everywhere. (Raywid 1989, p. 77)

Staff and Parent Evaluations

Dr. Raywid also surveyed and interviewed the teachers and consultants at the school, as well as the building and central administrators. Parents of interage program students anonymously filled out a questionnaire that asked how much they wanted to have their children in the program, how pleased they were with it, and how interested and enthusiastic their children seemed.

Ninety-five percent of the interage parents who responded found the program above average or excellent. Ninety-eight percent said their children seemed highly interested and committed to the program, and that same percent said their children were enthusiastic about going to school.

All the parents in the school also received letters inviting them to send statements to the investigator. This letter elicited only twelve responses, ten of which were critical of the program and pointed to admission policy, equity considerations, and the perceived separatist or elite attitude of the interage students. Some of these concerns were also voiced by some of the teachers. But in the questionnaire teachers received, thirteen of twenty-one teachers expressed an interest in working with colleagues to develop and operate their own vision of schooling.

The Raywid report also noted the pressures that The Interage Program placed on school and district administrators:

> It is they who have been the direct recipients of the parent pressure regarding IP placement, and of the dismay and protests of those whose youngsters have not been admitted. . . . (School) and district administrators are concerned about parent complaints and about teacher dissatisfactions. There is also an additional problem: public schools have increasingly pursued and at least implicitly assumed the desirability of uniformity and identical treatments. Although many of us are critical of bureaucracy in the abstract, probably even more of us have internalized its assumptions about what is appropriate and desirable in large scale public institutions. It is the bureaucratic assumption that fairness requires treating everyone in just the same way, which clearly underlies some of the criticisms expressed by teachers, parents and administrators (e.g., "For there to be in operation at a public school one program that is so completely different from three-fourths of the rest of the third grade population, is in my mind unfair, unreasonable and also undemocratic"). In an organization otherwise marked by units of identical size and composition and design, the administrative function is unquestionably complicated by the presence of one unit that is not comparable and for which standard operating procedures do not always fit. It is these two concerns—about dissatisfied populations, and about the administrative modifications and adaptations the IP necessitates, which seem most prominent in administrator discussion of the program. (Raywid 1989, p. 33)

Indeed, one might argue that these are the two most prominent administrative concerns of any innovation in any school setting. If there are teachers and parents who perceive inequity because of program differentiation, it is a problem not only for the administration but also for the program participants.

Today, there are fewer complaints about placement and equity. Because the program is now a fourth- and fifth-grade combination, there is, perhaps, less of an impact on the entire school. There are fewer children in The Interage Program. The students eat with their peer group and have after-lunch recess with them on the playground, so there is less perception that interage students are "different" or somehow separated from the rest of the school.

A Former Student's Evaluation

John Drango was one of our early graduates. He had joined the program as a fourth grader and spent three years in the interage classroom. He became an expert on the Civil War and returned to teach in our classroom when he was in high school. At the time of the evaluation, he wrote us a long letter. In a sense, he describes what it was like to be in this classroom better than anyone could. As we conclude our story, it seems fitting to let one of our students have the final say:

> I remember . . . having a difficult time finding my niche during the first couple of months of my first year in the program. . . . I also remember walking away from it three years later *knowing* that I had found myself. That's an enormous amount of growth in a short period of time, and it's a direct reflection of the fantastic kind of learning that went on inside the classroom. . . .
>
> What an environment it was! Constant stimulation from dozens of different "groups," lots of special instructors coming in to help out, 80 some odd different students (with 80 some odd different perspectives) . . . homemade plays and skits . . . students creating and leading their own groups . . . word puzzles circulating right and left . . . Chinese cooking instructions at lunch time from Lee Wong

. . . field trips to any number of places . . . options, options, options. We were bombarded with stimuli, and simply never had time to be bored or to fall into the tried-and-true but often dull patterns of a more standard education. . . .

I remember studying the Etruscans, Sacco and Vanzetti, Flow Charts and Other Bases, Trigonometry, Super Duper Spelling, Nader's Raiders, Madison Square Garden and dozens of other things. . . . My pace was interstellar. . . . I'll never forget asking my sister for math help one day, and seeing the stunned look on her face when she realized that I was studying the same "FOIL" method of algebra which she was studying in her eighth grade math class. . . .

The relationships formed during those years were very dynamic ones, borne of a common lust for learning and a shared knowledge that we were involved in something special. They are relationships that will always endure.

Further, the opportunity to befriend people of different ages was a unique and valuable experience. School children tend to be very parochial, I think, perceiving huge gulfs between themselves and children just a year or two removed in age. But . . . we were an inter-age operation all the way, enabling us to see each other more as friends and resources. That was a critical lesson to learn at a very early age. (John Drango 1988)

Appendix: Module Charts

	Monday	Tuesday	Wednesday	Thursday	Friday
9:30	Gym: Reds & Blues Music: Greens	Gym: Reds & Greens Music: Blues	Art: Reds Shop: Blues Science: Greens	Gym: Blues & Greens Music: Reds	LGM
10:15	Off to a Good Start News Broadcast Art Workshop Script Capitals	Shop: Trades Science: African Safari Anthropology Marsupials Greek Mythology	Number Theory	Shop: Trades Science: African Safari Anthropology Marsupials Greek Mythology	Number Theory
11:05	Children's Magazines Bookmarks & Bookplates Autumn Observers	Art: Collage *Mary Poppins* Mapping the USA Volcanoes and Earthquakes Picture Books	*Cam Jansen* *Aldo Applesause* Systems of the Body American Beginnings Poetry Potpourri	Art: Collage *Mary Poppins* Mapping the USA Volcanoes & Earthquakes Picture Books	*Cam Jansen* *Aldo Applesause* Systems of the Body American Beginnings Poetry Potpourri
12:00	Lunch	Lunch	Lunch	Lunch	Lunch
1:10	Let's Read READING AND CONFERENCES	Lib: Tomahawks, Drums, and Peacepipes *The Rats of Nimb* Let's Read READING AND CONFERENCES	*Ramona Quimby* Let's Read READING AND CONFERENCES	Lib: Tomahawks, Drums, and Peacepipes *The Rats of Nimb* Let's Read READING AND CONFERENCES	*Ramona Quimby* Let's Read READING AND CONFERENCES
2:15	*My Robot Buddy* Writers' Workshop Explorers Water Wonders & Worries	Number Theory	*My Robot Buddy* Writers' Workshop Explorers Water Wonders & Worries	Number Theory	Spelling

	Monday	Tuesday	Wednesday	Thursday	Friday
9:30	Gym: Blues & Reds Music: Greens	Gym: Greens & Reds Music: Blues	Art: Greens Shop: Reds Humanities: Blues	Gym: Blues & Greens Music: Reds	LGM
10:15	New Software Olympiad Practice Know Your Facts Freebies	Shop: Colonial Houses, Schools, Barns Science: Rock It to Me Making Sense of Logic *Konrad* Dinosaurs	Math	Shop: Colonial Houses, Schools, Barns Science: Rock It to Me Making Sense of Logic *Konrad* Dinosaurs	Math
11:05	Logo Riddles and Puzzles Faces of Freedom Know Your Facts Community	Art: Masks The Story of Germs Ancient Greece & Rome *Little Witch* Chemical Magic Watch Your Language	*Harriet the Spy* Unusual Animals India Fall into Winter Colonial Crafts	Art: Masks The Story of Germs Ancient Greece & Rome *Little Witch* Chemical Magic Watch Your Language Dinosaurs	*Harriet the Spy* Unusual Animals India Fall into Winter Colonial Crafts
12:00	Lunch	Lunch	Lunch	Lunch	Lunch
1:10	READING AND CONFERENCES	Lib: Think About It Creatures & Ghosts READING AND CONFERENCES	Reading Into Plays READING AND CONFERENCES	Lib: Life Skills Creatures & Ghosts READING AND CONFERENCES	Reactions Reading Into Plays READING AND CONFERENCES
2:15	Writers' Workshop Scripts Cultures *Aldo Ice Cream*	Math	Writers' Workshop Scripts Cultures *Aldo Ice Cream*	Math	Spelling

	Monday	Tuesday	Wednesday	Thursday	Friday
9:30	Gym: Blues & Reds Music: Greens	Gym: Greens & Reds Music: Blues	Art: Greens Music: Blues Humanities: Reds	Gym: Blues & Greens Music: Reds	LGM
10:15	Computers 1 The First Mammals Artists at Work Beg. Word Problems Food from the Field	Shop: Washington, DC Science: Halley's Comet Reading for Meaning Machines Mr. Popper's Penguins	Math CSMP	Shop: Washington, DC Science: Halley's Comet Reading for Meaning Machines Mr. Popper's Penguins	Math CSMPS
11:05	Computer 2 Sound Community Harder Words Problems Classy Classics	Art: Illustrious Illustrators Ancient Rome World Geography Poetry	The Revolutionary War Scripts How It's Made	Art: Illustrious Illustrators Ancient Rome World Geography Poetry	The Revolutionary War Scripts How It's Made
12:00	Lunch	Lunch	Lunch	Lunch	Lunch
1:10	Peace Great Stories News READING AND CONFERENCES	Lib: Illustrious Illustrators Washington Irving READING AND CONFERENCES	Logs Peace Reading into Plays READING AND CONFERENCES	Lib: Illustrious Illustrators Short Stories READING AND CONFERENCES	Logs The Mixed Up Files Reading into Plays Chess & Backgammon READING AND CONFERENCES
2:15	HMS Pinafore	Math Computation	HMS Pinafore	Math Computation	Spelling

	Monday	Tuesday	Wednesday	Thursday	Friday
9:30	Gym: Blues & Reds Music: Greens	Gym: Greens & Reds Music: Blues	Science: Blues Humanities: Greens Music: Reds	Gym: Blues & Greens Music: Reds	LGM
10:15	Metrics Israeli Dances *Tuck Everlasting* Books into Plays World Cooking	Shop: Long Island Science: The Invisible World Art Gallery Seeing the Light Plants *Behind the Attic Wall*	CSMP	Shop: Long Island Science: The Invisible World Art Gallery Seeing the Light Plants *Behind the Attic Wall*	CSMPS
11:05	World Cooking Family Trees Graphing Greats Minute Mysteries Me Myself & I	Art: Meet Matisse Literary Structures Reptiles & Amphibians Lincoln *The Lion, the Witch, & the Wardrobe*	Ancient Egypt Eskimos Canada The Law	Art: Meet Matisse Literary Structures Reptiles & Amphibians Lincoln *The Lion, the Witch, & the Wardrobe*	Ancient Egypt Eskimos Canada The Law
12:00	Lunch	Lunch	Lunch	Lunch	Lunch
1:10	Soup Famous Board Games *The Pushcart War*	Lib: The Afro-American Connection Wolves *Summer of the Swans*	Soup Famous Board Games *The Pushcart War*	Lib: The Afro-American Connection Stories of Famous People	Superstition Cloze Spelling Help
	READING AND CONFERENCES	READING AND CONFERENCES	READING AND CONFERENCES	READING AND CONFERENCES	READING AND CONFERENCES
2:15	HMS Pinafore Math	Math	HMS Pinafore Math	Math	Spelling

	Monday	Tuesday	Wednesday	Thursday	Friday
9:30	Gym: Blues & Reds Music: Greens	Gym: Greens & Reds Music: Blues	Shop: Greens Science: Reds Music: Blues	Gym: Blues & Greens Music: Reds	LGM
10:15	Calligraphy Plenty of Poetry How to Write a Report Nutrition	Shop: Colonial Signs Science: You Light Up My Life *I Juan de Pareja* *The Great Gilly Hopkins* Civil War Art Workshop	Math	Shop: Colonial Signs Science: You Light Up My Life *I Juan de Pareja* *The Great Gilly Hopkins* Civil War Art Workshop	Math
11:05	Script Sports Extra *Abel's Island* Storytime Plants	Art: Drawing Know Your Rights Exploring the Peninsula Knights & Castles Post It *The Upstairs Room*	Westward Ho! Creative Writing Energy Mayas, Incas, Aztecs	Art: Drawing Know Your Rights Exploring the Peninsula Knights & Castles Post It *The Upstairs Room*	Westward Ho! Creative Writing Energy Mayas, Incas, Aztecs
12:00	Lunch	Lunch	Lunch	Lunch	Lunch
1:10	Play Reading READING AND CONFERENCES	Lib: Truth is Stranger than Fiction READING AND CONFERENCES	Play Reading READING AND CONFERENCES	Lib: Truth is Stranger than Fiction READING AND CONFERENCES	READING AND CONFERENCES
2:15	Tall Tales Fables Myths & Legends *Akin's Secret Code* *The White Mountains*	Math	Tall Tales Fables Myths & Legends *Akin's Secret Code* *The White Mountains*	Math	Spelling

	Monday	Tuesday	Wednesday	Thursday	Friday
9:30	Gym: Blues & Reds Music: Greens	Gym: Greens & Reds Music: Blues	Shop: Blues Art: Reds Science: Greens	Gym: Blues & Greens Music: Reds	Movie Reviews Reading/Writing Stories Insects Stock Market Sniglets Close Encounters Pictures Magic
10:15	Computers: Basic French Calligraphy Story Poems Consumerism	Shop: Superstructures Science: Science Sleuths *The Secret Garden* Quilting Noticing Nature	Probability Geometry Multiplication & Division Notable Numbers	Shop: Superstructures Science: Science Sleuths *The Secret Garden* Quilting Noticing Nature	Probability Geometry Multiplication & Division Notable Numbers
11:05	Newsroom M.C. Escher Geography *Star Ka'at*	Art: Op Art Great Gorillas NY Times NY State	China The Middle East Homo Sapiens 20th Century USA	Art: Op Art Great Gorillas NY Times NY State	China The Middle East Homo Sapiens 20th Century USA
12:00	Lunch	Lunch	Lunch	Lunch	Lunch
1:10	READING AND CONFERENCES	Lib: The Brothers Grimm Braille READING AND CONFERENCES	I Juan de Pareja READING AND CONFERENCES	Lib: The Brothers Grimm READING AND CONFERENCES	I Juan de Pareja *Jonathan L. Seagull* READING AND CONFERENCES
2:15	Writing Workshop *Baseball Fever* A.A. Milne Camera Cubes	Arithmetricks Algebra Fractions Decimals & Percent	Writing Workshop *Baseball Fever* A.A. Milne Camera Cubes	Arithmetricks Algebra Fractions Decimals & Percent	Spelling

References

AIMS Education Foundation. Fresno, CA.

Atwell, N. 1987. *In the Middle*. Portsmouth, NH: Boynton/Cook.

Batterberry, M., and A. Ruskin. 1970. *Children's Homage to Picasso*. New York: Harry Abrams.

Blume, J. 1972. *Tales of a Fourth Grade Nothing*. New York: Dutton.

Bradbury, R. 1959. "All Summer in a Day." *A Medicine for Melancholy*. New York: Doubleday.

Bulla, C. R. 1975. *Shoeshine Girl*. New York: Crowell.

Burns, M. 1977. *I Hate Mathematics*. New York: Little, Brown.

Calkins, L. 1986. *The Art of Teaching Writing*. Portsmouth, NH: Heinemann.

Carroll, L. [1865] 1973. *Alice in Wonderland*. New York: Clarkson Potter.

Christopher, J. 1967. *The White Mountains*. New York: Macmillan.

Cobb, V. 1972. *Science Experiments You Can Eat*. New York: Lippincott.

Coerr, E. 1977. *Sadako and the Thousand Paper Cranes*. New York: Putnam.

Cohen, B. 1983. *Molly's Pilgrim*. New York: Lothrop, Lee and Shepard.

Collier, J., and C. Collier. 1987. *Jump Ship to Freedom*. New York: Dell.

de Trevino, E. 1965. *I, Juan de Pareja*. New York: Farrar, Straus and Giroux.

Dewey, J. 1897. "My Pedagogic Creed." *The Early Works of John Dewey 1895–1898*. Vol. 5. Carbondale, IL: Southern Illinois University Press.

———. 1899. *The School and Society*. Chicago: University of Chicago Press.

———. 1916. *Democracy and Education*. New York: Macmillan.

Drango, J. 1988. Letter to the author.

Estes, E. 1944. *The Hundred Dresses*. New York: Harcourt Brace.

Freire, P. 1994. *Pedagogy of Hope*. New York: Continuum.

Goodlad, J., and R. Anderson. 1963. *The Nongraded Elementary School*. New York: Harcourt, Brace and World.

Graves, D. 1983. *Writing: Teachers and Children at Work*. Portsmouth, NH: Heinemann.

Greene, M. 1980. "A Teacher Talks to Teachers." *Occasional Papers*. New York: Lincoln Center Institute.

Kerr, J. 1972. *When Hitler Stole Pink Rabbit*. New York: Coward McCann.

Kozol, J. 1991. *Savage Inequalities*. New York: Crown.

Kraus, R. 1971. *Leo the Late Bloomer*. New York: Windmill.

Lawson, R. 1951. *Ben and Me*. Boston: Little, Brown.

Lewis, C. S. 1950. *The Lion, the Witch, and the Wardrobe*. New York: Macmillan.

Lord, B. 1984. *In the Year of the Boar and Jackie Robinson*. New York: Harper and Row.

MacLachlan, P. 1985. *Sarah, Plain and Tall*. New York: Harper and Row.

Patterson, L. 1965. *Frederick Douglass: Freedom Fighter*. New York: Garrard.

Petry, A. 1955. *Harriet Tubman: Conductor on the Underground Railroad*. New York: Crowell.

Raywid, M. 1989. Report to the District. Great Neck, NY: Great Neck Public Schools.

Reiss, J. 1972. *The Upstairs Room*. New York: Crowell.

Sabartes, J. 1959. *Picasso: Variations on Velazquez' Painting "The Maids of Honor."* New York: Harry Abrams.

Snyder, Z. 1967. *The Egypt Game*. New York: Atheneum.

White, E. B. 1952. *Charlotte's Web*. New York: Harper.

Yashima, T. 1955. *Crow Boy*. New York: Viking.